tourism TATTLER

Issue 08 (AUGUST) 2015

PUBLISHER
Tourism Tattler (Pty) Ltd.
PO Box 891, Umhlanga Rocks, 4320
KwaZulu-Natal, South Africa.
Website: www.tourismtattler.com

EXECUTIVE EDITOR Des Langkilde
Cell: +27 (0)82 374 7260
Fax: +27 (0)86 651 8080
E-mail: editor@tourismtattler.com
Skype: tourismtattler

MAGAZINE ADVERTISING
ADVERTISING DIRECTOR Bev Langkilde
Cell: +27 (0)71 224 9971
Fax: +27 (0)86 656 3860
E-mail: bev@tourismtattler.com
Skype: bevtourismtattler

SUBSCRIPTIONS
http://eepurl.com/bocldD

BACK ISSUES (Click on the covers below).

▼ Jul 2015 ▼ Jun 2015 ▼ May 2015
▼ Apr 2015 ▼ Mar 2015 ▼ Feb 2015
▼ Jan 2015 ▼ Dec 2014 ▼ Nov 2014
▼ Oct 2014 ▼ Sep 2014 ▼ Aug 2014

Contents

14 BUSINESS: SA Tourism Review Report

35 MARKETING: Which SM Platform to Choose

I0469863

16 BUSINESS: Change for Tour Operators

38 RISK: Adventure Tourism

IN THIS ISSUE

EDITORIAL
04 Accreditation
05 Cover Story

ACCOLADES
06 2015 Lilizela Awards Finalists
08 Africa's Greenest Hotel

ATTRACTIONS
09 Cape Town's New7Wonder of Nature
10 Agritourism Tips for Tour Operators
11 South Coast Tourism Cuisine

BUSINESS
12 SATSA Market Intelligence Report
13 VAT in the Tourism Industry
14 SA Tourism Review Report
15 Skills Development Levy Refund
16 10 Tips to Embracing Change

COMPETITION
18 Win a Picnic Blanket

CONSERVATION
20 2015 Rhino Conservation Awards

EVENTS
24 Three Industries: One Event

HOSPITALITY
26 Property Profile - Mantis Collection
29 Waffling on about Waffles

LEGAL
24 The Law: Contracts - Part 13

MARKETING
32 Adventure Tourism Rankings
34 Adventure Tourism Growth
35 Which Social Media Platform?

NICHE TOURISM
36 Avitourism in South Africa

RISK
38 Risk in Adventure Tourism

TRADE NEWS
Visit our website at www.tourismtattler.com for daily travel trade news

EDITORIAL CONTRIBUTORS

Adv. Louis Nel   Jacques Maritz   Sharon House
Andrew Campbell   Leon Marais   Thomas Joubert
Charmaine Pratt   Lindsay de Heer   Tyne van der Merwe
Des Langkilde   Martin Jansen van Vuuren

MAGAZINE SPONSORS

02 SATIB Insurance Brokers
03 African Travel & Tourism Association
07 Mantis Collection
08 White Shark Projects
09 Table Mountain Aerial Cableway
10 Redberry Farm
11 Ugu South Coast Tourism
13 Sprout Consulting
15 Sprout Consulting
17 Travelogic
19 WYSTC 2015 - Cape Town
21 SATIB Conservation Trust
22 Sports & Events Tourism Exchange
23 WTM-London
25 SATIB Insurance Brokers
28 National Sea Rescue Institute (NSRI)
31 SATIB Insurance Brokers
35 SATIB Insurance Brokers
35 Sprout Consulting
40 kulula.com

Disclaimer: The Tourism Tattler is published by Tourism Tattler (Pty) Ltd and is the official trade journal of the Southern Africa Tourism Services Association (SATSA). The Tourism Tattler digital e-zine, is distributed free of charge to bona fide tourism stakeholders. Letters to the Editor are assumed intended for publication in whole or part and may therefore be used for such purpose. The information provided and opinions expressed in this publication are provided in good faith and do not necessarily represent the opinions of Tourism Tattler (Pty) Ltd, SATSA, its staff and its production suppliers. Advice provided herein should not be soley relied upon as each set of circumstances may differ. Professional advice should be sought in each instance. Neither Tourism Tattler (Pty) Ltd, SATSA, its staff and its production suppliers can be held legally liable in any way for damages of any kind whatsoever arising directly or indirectly from any facts or information provided or omitted in these pages or from any statements made or withheld or from supplied photographs or graphic images reproduced by the publication.

Would you trust your insurance broker with your life?

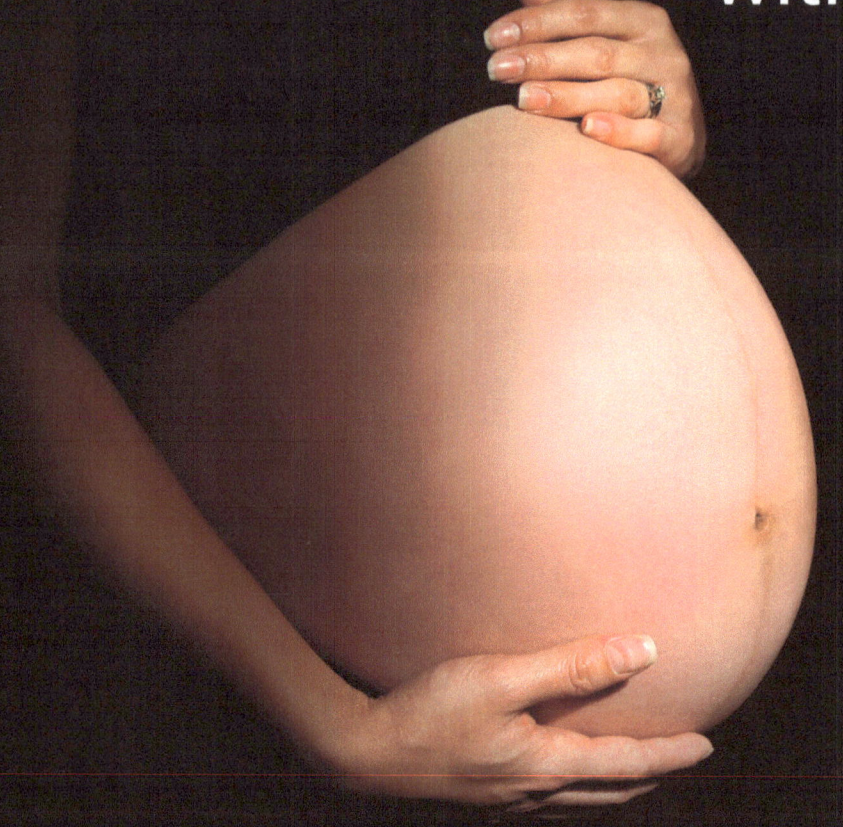

Lauren & David decided to spend a weekend away in the Drakensberg. Shortly after arrival at their hotel, Lauren started to feel cramping in her lower abdomen which continuously worsened into the evening. The hotel staff immediately contacted SATIB24 Crisis Call. Our doctor discussed the presenting features of Lauren's condition with David and attributed the sudden pain pointing to a potentially life threatening scenario - ectopic pregnancy.

Whilst the doctor was consulting with David, the nearest private ambulance provider was contacted and a response vehicle and ambulance requested. The receiving doctor of the nearest private hospital was informed by our doctor of the suspected diagnoses and requested an emergency admittance for Lauren. She was stabilised by a response

paramedic and evacuated with advanced life support to the private hospital where she was admitted and treated for an ectopic pregnancy. Had it not been for the quick initiative & careful planning, even a mere 10 minutes delay may have resulted in Lauren's demise.

SATIB24 Crisis Call is a critical incident management service with an insurance component available *ONLY* to SATIB clients. Staffed by a professional team who manage a variety of critical incidents on a daily basis, they know what the issues are, where the exposures lie and how best to manage any critical incident on the continent of Africa. We deal with an average of 10 incidents daily! Don't wait until it is too late - *Call us NOW!*

SATIB CONSERVATION TRUST
WILDLIFE & COMMUNITIES

For more information, please contact us on:
T 0861 SATIB 4U (72842 48) | **E** info@satib.co.za

  www.satib.com

SATIB Insurance Brokers Pty (Ltd) is an authorised Financial Services Provider. FSP License No. 16388/ IGF No. 002366. Compliance Officer: National Compliance CC Practice No 1307

PROMOTING TOURISM TO
AFRICA
FROM ALL CORNERS OF THE WORLD

Recognised as the Voice of African Tourism, Atta reaches across 22 countries in Africa, showcasing over 530 elite buyers and suppliers of African tourism product.

- Leading role at trade shows around the world
- Networking opportunities
- Industry representation on international commitees & the media
- Interactive platform for information & education
- Daily news service on all aspects of African tourism
- Network of specialist consultants

Join our knowledgeable and experienced membership to increase awareness and visibility of your company

f attatourism | www.atta.travel | info@atta.travel **y** @atta_tourism

Lead Sponsor | Working in partnership with Atta

SOUTH AFRICAN AIRWAYS

A STAR ALLIANCE MEMBER

Accreditation

The African Travel & Tourism Association (Atta)

Tel: +44 20 7937 4408 • Email: info@atta.travel • Website: www.atta.travel

Members in 22 African countries and 37 worldwide use Atta to: Network and collaborate with peers in African tourism; Grow their online presence with a branded profile; Ask and answer specialist questions and give advice; and Attend key industry events.

National Accommodation Association of South Africa (NAA-SA)

Tel: +2786 186 2272 • Fax: +2786 225 9858 • Website: www.naa-sa.co.za

The NAA-SA is a network of mainly smaller accommodation providers around South Africa – from B&Bs in country towns offering comfortable personal service to luxurious boutique city lodges with those extra special touches – you're sure to find a suitable place, and at the same time feel confident that your stay at an NAA-SA member's establishment will meet your requirements.

Regional Tourism Organisation of Southern Africa (RETOSA)

Tel: +2711 315 2420/1 • Fax: +2711 315 2422 • Website: www.retosa.co.za

RETOSA is a Southern African Development Community (SADC) institution responsible for tourism growth and development. RETOSA's aims are to increase tourist arrivals to the region through. RETOSA Member States are Angola, Botswana, DR Congo, Lesotho, Madagascar, Malawi, Mauritius, Mozambique, Namibia, Seychelles, South Africa, Swaziland, Tanzania, Zambia and Zimbabwe.

Southern Africa Tourism Services Association (SATSA)

Tel: +2786 127 2872 • Fax: +2711 886 755 • Website: www.satsa.com

SATSA is a credibility accreditation body representing the private sector of the inbound tourism industry. SATSA members are Bonded thus providing a financial guarantee against advance deposits held in the event of the involuntary liquidation. SATSA represents: Transport providers, Tour Operators, DMC's, Accommodation Suppliers, Tour Brokers, Adventure Tourism Providers, Business Tourism Providers and Allied Tourism Services providers.

Southern African Vehicle Rental and Leasing Association (SAVRALA)

Contact: manager@savrala.co.za • Website: w

Founded in the 1970's, SAVRALA is the representative voice of Southern Africa's vehicle rental, leasing and fleet management sector. Our members have a combined national footprint with more than 600 branches countrywide. SAVRALA are instrumental in steering industry standards and continuously strive to protect both their members' interests, and those of the public, and are therefore widely respected within corporate and government sectors.

Seychelles Hospitality & Tourism Association (SHTA)

Tel: +248 432 5560 • Fax: +248 422 5718 • Website: www.shta.sc

The Seychelles Hospitality and Tourism Association was created in 2002 when the Seychelles Hotel Association merged with the Seychelles Hotel and Guesthouse Association. SHTA's primary focus is to unite all Seychelles tourism industry stakeholders under one association in order to be better prepared to defend the interest of the industry and its sustainability as the pillar of the country's economy.

International Coalition of Tourism Partners (ICTP)

Website: www.tourismpartners.org

ICTP is a travel and tourism coalition of global destinations committed to Quality Services and Green Growth.

International Institute for Peace through Tourism

Website: www.iipt.org

IIPT is dedicated to fostering tourism initiatives that contribute to international understanding and cooperation.

OTM India 2015

Website: www.otm.co.in

OTM is India's biggest travel trade show, in the largest travel market in India – Mumbai.

The Safari Awards

Website: www.safariawards.com

Safari Award finalists are amongst the top 3% in Africa and the winners are unquestionably the best.

World Travel Market

WTM Africa - Cape Town in April, WTM Latin America - São Paulo in April, and WTM - London in November. WTM is the place to do business.

World Youth Student and Educational (WYSE) Travel Confederation

Website: www.wysetc.org

WYSE is a global not-for-profit membership organisation.

World Travel Awards

Website: www.worldtravelawards.com

Established in 1993 WTA rewards the very best in travel. WTA's global media partner network has a monthly readership of 1.7 million and a TV audience reach of 90 million.

World Luxury Hotel Awards

Website: www.luxuryhotelawards.com

World Luxury Hotel Awards is an international company that provides award recognition to the best hotels from all over the world.

Adventure tourism is a sector of the travel industry that our August edition cover sponsor, SATIB Insurance Brokers have specialised in for many years.

Obtaining tailor-made liability risk transfer cover for adventure operators is no easy task, considering the diversity of potentially hazardous activities that are offered by adventure tourism operators

To compound matters, inbound tourists emanating from European Union countries are protected by the European Community Directive 90/314/EEC on Package Holidays and Travel Trade Act, 1995, which places the onus of liability squarely on the shoulders of the travel organiser who sold the package to the tourist – from the time of departure to return.

For more detail on the EC Directive, download the SATSA Southern Africa Tourism Insurance Directive PDF booklet at *www.satib.com*.

Given the onerous terms of the EC Directive, it's understandable that buyers insist that their ground handlers in Africa, and specifically their activity service suppliers, such as adventure operators, have appropriate liability insurance cover in place that not only complies with the terms of the Directive but also extends to cover all sub-contractors involved in the performance and delivery of the package holiday.

So important is this aspect of liability, that South Africa's previous Minister of Tourism, Marthinus van Schalkwyk made a call for the sector to put sound regulatory measures relating to safety and operational standards in place, in order to build the credibility and

profile of a reliable Adventure Tourism industry in South Africa.

The National Department of Tourism (NDT) partnered with the South African Tourism Services Association (SATSA) to organise and host an inaugural workshop on self-regulation for the Adventure Tourism Sector which took place on the 19 March 2014 in Cape Town. The workshop provided a platform for information sharing, exchange of best practices, and solicited input pertaining to the implementation of stakeholder consultative sessions to be organised throughout the 2015 financial year. *(read more on the subject of adventure tourism on pages 32, 34, 38 and 39).*

In this edition of Tourism Tattler, we salute Africa's Greenest Hotel, and share the achievements of the 2015 Lilizela Tourism Award finalists, and the 2015 Rhino Conservation Award winners.

We also cover the recently released report on recommendations to guide South African Tourism's future strategic direction. We also have tips on Agritourism and on managing operational change for Tour Operators.

There's business advise on Value Added Tax and on how to claim money back from Skills Development Levy contributions. Several restaurant and property reviews, and finally tips for those who want to attract the growing Avitourism market to South Africa. i**t**

Enjoy your reading!

Yours in Tourism,

Des Langkilde. *editor@tourismtattler.com*

TAKE A BREAK

Go to **BidorBuy.co.za** this August and bid for a two-night all-inclusive voucher at any one of three **Mantis Collection** luxury properties.
See pages 26 to 27.

2015 Lilizela Tourism Award Finalists

Congratulations to the 2015 Lilizela Tourism Award finalists. Their achievement represents recognition from both their clients, and the travel trade at large for their respective commitment to service excellence and innovation, which contributes to growing South Africa's global destination competitiveness, writes **Des Langkilde**.

The 2015 Lilizela Tourism Award finalists can be viewed on the official website at _www.lilizela.co.za_

This year's 329 finalists represent just over one third (34%) of the 934 entries received for the 2015 awards, which reflects the high standards set by the adjudication process. _Note that this analysis excludes the Imvelo Award entries, which closes on 14 August._

In terms of the number of entries submitted by province, the Eastern Cape had the most, followed by the Western Cape, with KwaZulu-Natal and Gauteng at almost identical numbers.

The number of finalists by province though, reflects the quality of entries, which is what the Lilizela Tourism Awards is all about. In this regard, the Western Cape takes the lead, followed by the Eastern Cape and Gauteng, as shown in the table below.

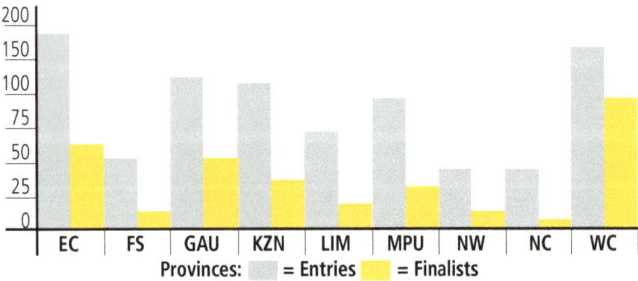

The overall entry numbers indicate that establishment owners want recognition and reward for offering excellent products and services. Notable this year, is an increase in the number of Small to Micro Enterprises (SMEs) who participated. This is important, as local SMEs are the backbone of South Africa's tourism industry and constitutes a segment that the Lilizela Tourism Awards aims to help grow and flourish.

However, the gap between the number of entries received and the number of establishments and tourist products that exist in the country, still remains.

For the Lilizela Tourism Awards to be truly representative of quality and service excellence in South Africa's tourism landscape, more tourism products and establishments must enter to be judged.

As Thulani Nzima, Chief Executive Officer at South African Tourism says; "We will continue to drive awareness about the awards and their benefit to the domestic tourism landscape but still rely on the public endorsement from industry members who have participated."

About the Awards

Lilizela is an _Nguni_ word, which means to ululate: a uniquely African act of congratulating work well done. Lilizela is a name that truly distinguishes this uniquely South African award.

The Lilizela Tourism Awards have been running for three successful years and is an initiative of the National Department of Tourism (NDT) and delivered by the Tourism Grading Council of South Africa (TGCSA). The award winners are selected based on the feedback provided by guests, TripAdvisor guest reviews and through the deliberation of a panel of judges.

The award process follows four steps, namely; NOMINATING / ENTRY, VOTING, JUDGING and AWARDING.

The travel industry and, more importantly, the consumers of products and services offered by South Africa's tourism industry, are invited to vote for tourism businesses via the website at _www.lilizela.co.za_. _Note that only tourist guides are nominated, everyone else enters._

Entries are made under 4 Focus Areas reflecting 8 Categories with the 9th Category being the Minister's Award.

The results recognise the best of the best of business owners and service providers who uphold service of excellence in their day to day operations, and the finalists bolster South Africa's reputation as a destination of excellence and variety across all experiences and accommodation types.

One seldom gives thought to the effort and logistics involved behind the scenes in putting together an annual industry award, specifically one which aims to recognise and reward the diversity of tourism players and businesses who work passionately and with pride to deliver world-class products and services, and whose delivery grows South Africa's global destination competitiveness.

In my opinion, the organisers and hosts of the Lilizela Tourism Awards - including each provisional tourism authority - can be justifiably proud of their collective efforts in terms of transparency, fairness in the adjudication process and organisation of the award ceremony events, which are akin to the film industry's Oscar Awards, with regional award ceremonies convened in each of South Africa's nine provinces during September and the final national event held in Johannesburg in October. **it**

2015 PROVINCIAL AWARDS CEREMONY DATES		
PROVINCE	**DATE**	**CITY**
Northern Cape	02 September	Kimbereley/Upington
Free State	03 September	Bloemfontein
Western Cape	04 September	Cape Town Central
Mpumalanga	08 September	Mbombela
Eastern Cape	10 September	Port Elizabeth
Bokone Bophirima	11 September	TBC
KwaZulu Natal	16 September	Durban/PMB
Gauteng	22 September	TBC
Limpopo	26 September	Phalaborwa

The National Awards will take place on 22 October 2015 in Johannesburg.

Bush Lodge | Amakhala Game Reserve | Eastern Cape | Near Port Elizabeth

Oceana Beach & Wildlife Reserve | Eastern Cape | Near Port Alfred

HillsNek Safari Camp | Amakhala Game Reserve | Eastern Cape | Near Port Elizabeth

Unearthing the Exceptional

From the World's finest Hotels, Lodges, Eco-Escapes, Lifestyle Resorts & eXtreme Holidays, Mantis is synonymous with quality, excellence and distinction – a brand that will go beyond every expectation.

Tel: +27 (0) 41 404 9300 | info@mantiscollection.com | www.mantiscollection.com

mantis

Hotels, Eco-Escapes
& Lifestyle Resorts

Africa's Greenest Hotel Attains Global First Certification

Hotel Verde's management and staff toasting their collective achievement of a second LEED Platinum Green Building Certificate.

On 2 June 2015 Hotel Verde was awarded a second LEED (Leadership in Energy & Environmental Design) Platinum Green Building Certificate by the United States Green Building Council, making it the world's only hotel to achieve double-platinum status. LEED is a green building certification programme recognising best-in-class building strategies.

On 23 May 2014 Hotel Verde had achieved a Platinum rating under the LEED green building rating system in the category of Building Design and Construction and is the first building in Africa to have been certified as such.

Adding to the hotel's already impressive array of accolades, Hotel Verde was awarded the global Green Hotelier of 2015, Africa and the Middle East award. In 2014, the hotel was awarded the distinction of being the 'World's Best City Hotel' by the World Responsible Tourism Awards 2014.

Read more on Hotel Verde's Platinum Green Building Certification story online at *www.tourismtattler.com/?p=59619*

Sharing their Green Building 'thrivability' expertise

Hotel Verde's General Manager, Samantha Annandale coined the phrase 'thrivability' at a presentation that I attended during WTMAfrica in Cape Town. Samantha defined 'thrivability' as "Hospitality solutions that are not only sustainable but Thrivable: incorporating people, profit and planet. The language of sustainability is about neutralising. Thrivability is about succeeding."

Announcing their expansion plans into Africa through a new division known as Verde Hotels, Samantha shared some interesting facts – an unusual act of transparency not often divulged by hoteliers.

In comparing and quantifying the Return On Investment (ROI) between building a green hotel versus a traditional hotel, she said that Hotel Verde's flagship project located in Cape Town International Airport's industrial zone, cost R187 million to build, which included the premium for building green, compared to R1.15 million per key without the green technology premium. An average traditional hotel will cost on average between R1.3 to R1.5 million per key without the green technology.

Isolating quantifiable ROI's, the green build project gained just over R30 million. in free press exposure since the project commenced, reduced utility consumption costs by 70% (cost per room night based on utilities at Hotel Verde is R29.52 vs an average Cape Town hotel of R97.28 cost), and lowered energy consumption by 70,79% (77 kWh/sqm/annum vs Cape Town hotel average of 255 kWh/sqm/annum), which even beat the LEED model average of 144 kWh/sqm/annum by 46,53%.

Overall, the Hotel Verde green-build project resulted in 35% lower operating costs, a 70% reduction in energy consumption, 85% waste to landfill reduction, and 35% lower water consumption.

"It is the strong belief of the Verde Hotels team and myself that the hotel industry has changed, and that we simply cannot build or operate hotels in the same way that we have done for the past twenty years. Verde Hotels is the future of hospitality. Companies with proactive environmental strategies have a 4% higher return on investment, 9% higher sales growth and 17% higher operating growth than companies with poor environmental track records," said Samantha.

As a hotel management company, Verde Hotels aims to spearhead sustainable hotel management throughout Africa by offering hotel investors and developers property management packages for both new construction projects and retrofitting of existing buildings.

For more information visit www.verdehotels.co.za or www.hotelverde.co.za or email bookings @hotelverde.co.za

EXPERIENCE ADRENALINE

FAIR TRADE TOURISM

SATSA
Southern Africa Tourism
Services Association
BONDED

WHITE SHARK PROJECTS

+27 (0)28 384 1774 | bookings@whitesharkprojects.co.za | www.whitesharkprojects.co.za

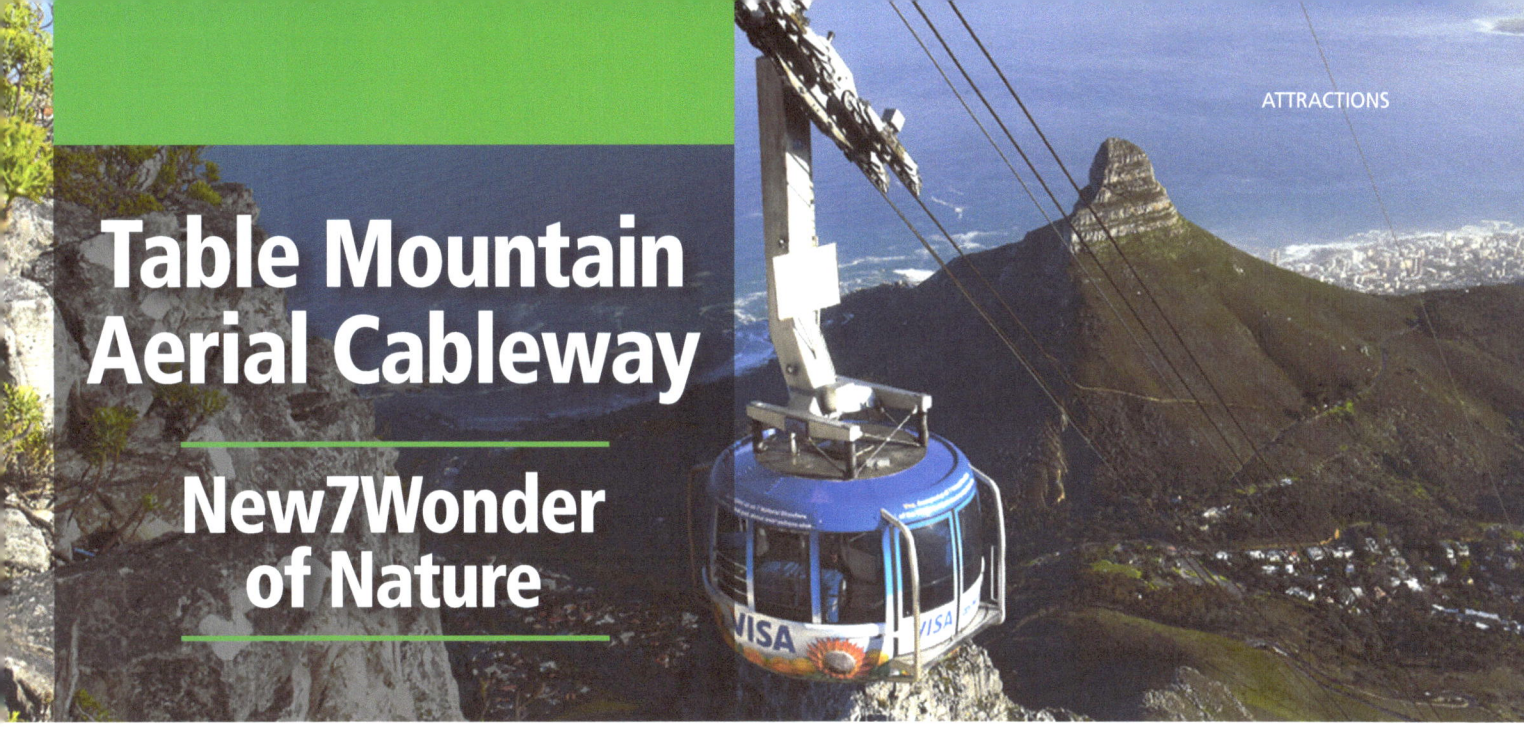

Table Mountain Aerial Cableway

New7Wonder of Nature

The best views of Cape Town are seen from the top of Table Mountain, an official New7Wonder of Nature. The Cableway takes visitors to the summit of Table Mountain in less than 5 minutes, and the cable car's rotating floor ensures that all visitors get a 360 degree aerial view of the city.

Once on top, one has a view of the Cape Town city centre, Table Bay, Robben Island, Lion's Head and Devil's Peak, the Cape Flats out towards Khayelitsha and Mitchell's Plain, the Hottentots Holland Mountains and even across the Table Mountain range towards Cape Point. 2km of pathways lead visitors to many vantage points to enjoy the views and tranquility. The Lower Station and Upper Cable Station, as well as its pathways, are wheelchair friendly.

Short guided walks depart from the Twelve Apostles Terrace on the hour from 9h00 to 15h00. The guided walks are offered free of charge. Visitor facilities at the Top Station include The Shop at the Top and the Table Mountain Café. The unique and interesting shop offers a wide variety of souvenirs and gifts to keep the entire family happy. The Table Mountain Café is open for breakfast, lunch and refreshments. Meals may be complemented with a selection of fine wines.

Cableway tickets can be purchased online or from the ticket office. The Cableway operates weather permitting. For information call +27 (0)21 424 8181 or visit www.tablemountain.net   it

Table Mountain was officially named one of the official New7Wonders of Nature on 11 November 2011.

tsi
TOURISM SAFETY INITIATIVE

REPORT TOURISM CRIMES

0861 tsi 874 911

www.tourismsafety.co.za

★ **Police: 10111**

✚ **Emergency Services: 10177**

🚌 **Road Traffic Info: 084 303 0345**

ℹ **Tourism & Travel Info: 083 123 6789**

📞 **Telephone Directory: 1023**

TABLE MOUNTAIN
OFFICIAL NEW 7 WONDER OF NATURE
new7wonders.com

DISCOVER TABLE MOUNTAIN

Access Table Mountain via the Cableway and explore our New 7 Wonder of Nature. Enjoy spectacular views, guided walks and wander around the Cape Floral Kingdom. Also take time out to enjoy the Table Mountain Café and Shop @ the Top.

Tel: +27 21 424 8181
info@tablemountain.net
Tickets available at
www.tablemountain.net

 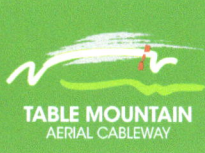

TABLE MOUNTAIN
AERIAL CABLEWAY

Agritourism Tips for Tour Operators

Redberry Farm opened in 2000, and fifteen years down the line run a successful **agritourism** business alongside their commercial fruit production. In this article **Sharon House** provides a few tips for Tour Operators to arrange successful agri-tour groups.

When is a good time to visit a farm?

At Redberry Farm, agri-tours are offered all year round because they produce winter strawberries too. However, for the best berries, tours are recommended from the end of August until December as this is their traditional strawberry season.

How to make a booking?

Tour operators can conveniently view the different packages that Redberry Farm offers on their website. It is best to book via telephone to secure preferred dates and times as they only take one group in the morning and one group in the afternoon per day. Their tours are for a minimum of 10 people, but they can accommodate bigger groups in excess of 100 people.

Once a package has been selected and the date and time confirmed, Redberry ask for pre-payment. This is to make arrival on the day seamless and avoids awkward paying arrangements before the tour can begin.

What happens on arrival?

Busses are parked on the field area so that the bus has enough space to manoeuvre. The bus driver is welcome to stretch his legs and relax in the tea garden while the group proceed with their tour.

Upon arrival, the tour leader should check in at the Farm Stall. A host will welcome you and take you to the area where the briefing part of the tour is conducted. Once everyone is settled in, a welcome strawberry juice is served. The presenter – either the farm manager or owner – will begin his interactive talk and discussion.

Thereafter the presenter will distribute the strawberry picking containers and escort the group to the miniature train where they will be transported in groups of 15 people to the strawberry fields. The group then roam the fields to fill their containers with fresh strawberries. Picking fields do vary though, depending on where the best ripe fruit is available, so the train ride may take place either before or after the picking. On average, the whole tour process takes one hour. If the tour package selected includes the hedge maze adventure and a meal, this will occur in the order that has been arranged upon booking (depending on the time of day). The hedge maze takes one to two hours to complete and about half an hour should be allowed for meals.

What agri-tours does the farm offer?

The standard one hour agri-tour at Redberry Farm, called a "Talk & Tour" is very affordable – starting at R72 for adults and R53 for children (2015 rack rate). It consists of a welcome strawberry juice on arrival, an interesting talk and discussion, strawberry picking in the fields and a miniature train ride. The talk explains how strawberries are grown, different varieties available in the world and region, and interesting general facts.

The farm is equipped with catering and other activities so if you have time, your group can easily enjoy a half day. Their hedge maze is the largest in the Southern Hemisphere and the objective is to find all seven strawberry stations. Anyone who manages to do this, will have "discovered the strawberry secrets", as each station has an educational board with information about strawberry propagation, ancient legends and modern day health uses. For group catering, platters, scones or good quality hamburgers are available.

Where is the farm located?

Redberry Farm is located just off the R404 – the traditional route to Oudtshoorn and the Cango Caves – and 4km from George airport, making them conveniently positioned for groups who want to hop back on to the N2, as Mossel Bay is just a half hour drive away. Redberry Farm, as a tourist attraction, is rated as number two on Trip Advisor under 'Things to do in George' and has been awarded a Certificate of Excellence.

Hestie Crous-Beckett, Managing Director at Agricultural Tours Worldwide, has been sending tours to Redberry Farm for a number of years and recommends the experience: *"I always enjoy doing business with Redberry Farm as they have provided me with excellent service and the tourists have always enjoyed their visit to the farm. I always try and include a visit to them."* i**t**

For more information visit www.redberryfarm.co.za

School, family & agricultural tours

044 870 7123 | George, GARDEN ROUTE

Redberry farm

www.redberryfarm.co.za

South Coast Tourism
Cuisine

There's more to the South Coast of KwaZulu-Natal in South Africa, than just the activities and attractions that I've reported on previously - there's the food too, writes **Des Langkilde**.

In the June edition I wrote about the activities that I experienced during my jam-packed post-Indaba media FAM trip itinerary hosted by Ugu South Coast Tourism. Namely Fun Boat Rides with C-Freaks, Beach Horse Rides with Selsdon Park Estate, and Zip Lines with Lake Eland Game Reserve. In July, the attractions, namely S'khumba Crafts, Pistols Saloon, and Mac Banana. This month, I'll cover the best part of any tourism destination – the food!

The Waffle House

If you think waffles are just for desserts – think again! The Waffle House in Ramsgate has turned the humble waffle into a culinary art. From breakfast toppings to savoury or sweet toppings, their waffles are available in gluten, dairy and egg free options. *Baaie Lekker!*

*Read our **Restaurant Review** on **page 29** in this edition.*

Visit www.wafflehouse.co.za or to book call +27 (0)39 314 9424.

Blue Lagoon Restaurant

Situated on Ramsgate's blue flag beach, the Blue Lagoon Restaurant is apparently renowned by locals for its seafood menu. As the evening when I visited was a bit chilly, I ignored the seafood and opted instead for the Oxtail with mash, which was tender and perfectly spiced in a rich red wine sauce. My colleagues opted for the 500g rump steak, and the Eisbein, which is grilled crispy, and served with mash and sauerkraut. This restaurant's recipe for success; location (right on the beach), atmosphere, fantastic food, value for money menu, and efficient service.

For reviews see TripAdvisor or to book call +27 (0)39 314 4149.

Leopards Rock Lookout Chalets, Coffee Shop / Restaurant

Leopard Rock Lookout's restaurant deck overlooks the spectacular Umzimkulu River Valley at Oribi Gorge – a perfect setting for homemade country fare, prepared by hosts Sue and Andries Bruwer. Unfortunately I missed dinner and lunch, but the English breakfast

(included in the accommodation rate) was a wholesome serving – it comes with sausages, bacon, eggs, toast, tomatoes – *the works!*

Visit www.leopardrockc.co.za or to book call +27 (0)74 124 0902.

Next month I'll be reporting on accommodation options along the KZN South Coast - or rather those that I stayed at. **it**

IT'S PARADISE

South Coast
PARADISE OF THE ZULU KINGDOM

www.tourismsouthcoast.co.za

Head Office +27(0)39-682-7944
Scottburgh +27(0)39-976-1364
Hibberdene +27(0)39-699-3203
Umzumbe +27(0)61-443-4539
Ezingoleni / Oribi +27(0)39-687-7561
Harding / Ingeli +27(0)39 553 0012
Shelly Centre +27(0)39-315-7065
Margate +27(0)39-312-2322
Southbroom +27(0)39-316-6139
Munster / Port Edward +27(0)39-319-1193

SATSA
Southern Africa Tourism Services Association
BONDED*

Grant Thornton

Market Intelligence Report

The information below was extracted from data available as at **01 AUGUST 2015**. By **Martin Jansen van Vuuren** of **Grant Thornton**.

ARRIVALS

The latest available data from **Statistics South Africa** is for **January to March 2015*:**

	Current period	Change over same period last year
UK	129 149	5.2%
Germany	85 254	-3.1%
USA	64 125	-7.9%
India	17 079	-12.6%
China (incl Hong Kong)	19 144	-37.8%
Overseas Arrivals	589 802	-6.8%
African Arrivals	1 699 531	-5.6%
Total Foreign Arrivals	2 292 169	-5.9%

HOTEL STATS

The latest available data from **STR Global** is for **January to June 2015**:

Current period	Average Room Occupancy (ARO)	Average Room Rate (ARR)	Revenue Per Available Room (RevPAR)
All Hotels in SA	61.1%	R 1 082	R 661
All 5-star hotels in SA	62.0%	R 1 970	R 1 222
All 4-star hotels in SA	60.3%	R 1 020	R 614
All 3-star hotels in SA	60.3%	R 867	R 523
Change over same period last year			
All Hotels in SA	0.4%	6.1%	6.5%
All 5-star hotels in SA	0.0%	8.7%	8.6%
All 4-star hotels in SA	0.6%	5.4%	6.0%
All 3-star hotels in SA	-1.4%	7.2%	5.7%

ACSA DATA

The latest available data from **ACSA** is for **January to June 2015**:

Change over same period last year	Passengers arriving on International Flights	Passengers arriving on Regional Flights	Passengers arriving on Domestic Flights
OR Tambo International	-1.7%	-4.2%	7.8%
Cape Town International	7.9%	6.5%	6.3%
King Shaka International	-4.0%	N/A	3.5%

CAR RENTAL DATA

The latest available data from **SAVRALA** is for **January to March 2015**:

	Current period	Change over same period last year
Industry rental days	4 373 919	-2%
Industry utilisation	71.8%	-1.5%
Industry Average daily revenue	1 352 463 563	1%

WHAT THIS MEANS FOR MY BUSINESS

The data from Statistics South Africa shows the continued decline in foreign tourist arrivals. This trend is echoed in the ACSA data, which shows a decline in passengers arriving on international and regional flights, although Cape Town International Airport is bucking the trend with strong growth from both international and regional flights. Passengers arriving on domestic flights continue to grow strongly indicating that domestic business tourism is recovering.

Note that African Arrivals plus Overseas Arrivals do not add to Total Foreign Arrivals due to the exclusion of unspecified arrivals, which could not be allocated to either African or Overseas.

For more information contact Martin at Grant Thornton on +27 (0)21 417 8838 or visit: http://www.gt.co.za

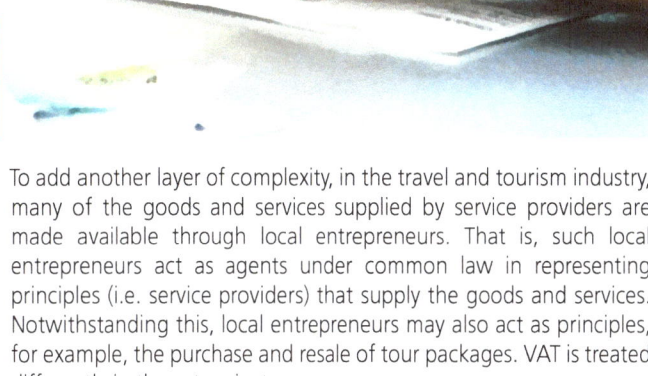

VAT
in the
Tourism
Industry

Value Added Tax (VAT) charged to clients in the Tourism Industry can be a mine field, writes **Thomas Joubert**.

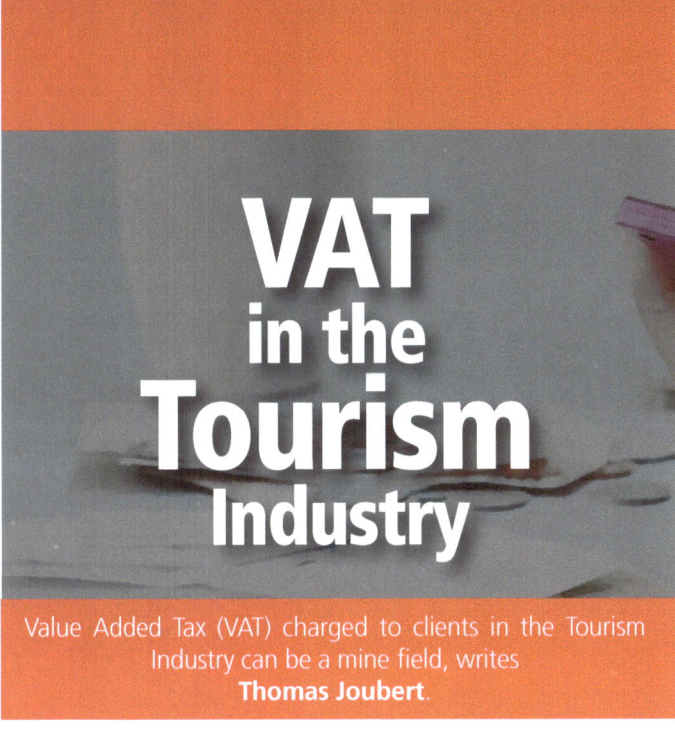

In the tourism industry, not only does one need to look at the costs of putting together the trip, where there may be different VAT treatments for using your own vehicle, using a transport company or hiring a vehicle, but things get even further complicated if your company has foreign tourists.

Determining whether you have to charge VAT on the fee for arranging the trip for foreign tourists depends on where your foreign guests are at the time that your business arranges their trip to South Africa.

The fees or commission charged by the your local business for arranging the foreign tourist's trip is zero-rated according to section 11(2)(ℓ) of the VAT Act if the foreign tourist and your business are outside South Africa at the time the service of arranging the tour package for the foreign tourist is rendered.

On the other hand, the fees or commission charged by the your local business for arranging the foreign tourist's trip is standard-rated according to section 7(1)(a) of the VAT Act if the foreign tourist and your business are in South Africa at the time the service of arranging the tour package is for the foreign tourist is rendered.

To add another layer of complexity, in the travel and tourism industry, many of the goods and services supplied by service providers are made available through local entrepreneurs. That is, such local entrepreneurs act as agents under common law in representing principles (i.e. service providers) that supply the goods and services. Notwithstanding this, local entrepreneurs may also act as principles, for example, the purchase and resale of tour packages. VAT is treated differently in these two instances.

The above just lightly touches on some of the issues to consider when putting together an itinerary and how to calculate the correct VAT. If you charge VAT on items that you shouldn't, it will make you more expensive than your competitors who are treating it correctly. If you are not charging VAT on items you should, then SARS could levy an additional 14% without you being able to claim it back from clients.

This is thus an area that you need to read up on and ensure that your bookkeeper/accountant is up to speed on. Spout Consulting offers a retainer service to advise on the correct treatment of VAT. i𝐭

For more info contact Thomas at *thomas@sproutconsulting.co.za*.

if this is your understanding
of VAT...
...we need to talk!

The issue of VAT in the Tourism Industry follows a specific set of rules and regulations. Sprout Consulting can assist you in ascertaining that you have accounted for and correctly applied the VAT rules and regulations when invoicing. We will help with the following:

- VAT Guidance
- Submission of objections and appeals

Sprout Consulting would like to make sure your invoicing is compliant with current regulations for a monthly retainer, contact us to find out more!

H R | M A R K E T I N G | A C C O U N T I N G | I T

info@sproutconsulting.co.za | **www.sproutconsulting.co.za** f

sprout
CONSULTING
your outsourced head office

SA Tourism Review Report

A panel of experts have reviewed how South African Tourism is responding to the dynamics of the national and international tourism sector and has made recommendations to guide its future strategic direction, writes **Des Langkilde**.

Chairman of the SA Tourism Review Committee, Valli Moosa handing over the Report to Minister Derek Hanekom.
Image: tourism.gov.za

The SA Tourism Review Committee appointed by the Minister of Tourism, Derek Hanekom, in February 2015 to review the mandate, functioning, institutional and governance arrangements of SA Tourism has been released. The Committee was comprised of Mavuso Msimang (Director at SAAB Grintek / CEO at SANParks) , Tanya Abrahamse (CEO at SANBI), Nunu Ntshingila-Njeke (Chairman at Ogilvy South Africa), Kate Rivett-Carnac (Kate Rivett-Carnac Consulting), Jeanine Pires (Brazilian Ministry - 2016 Olympic and Paralympic Games), Crispian Olver as Deputy Chair (CEO at Linkd Environmental Services), and Chaired by Valli Moosa (Chairman of Sun International Limited).

Announcing the release of the report, Minister Hanekom said "I am satisfied that the review panel has achieved its objectives and fulfilled its mandate. The panel's recommendations will help the country to grow its competitive edge in the global tourism marketplace, and will also promote domestic tourism."

The report 'SA Tourism Review: Report of the Expert Panel, June 2015' states that "The overwhelming majority of stakeholders surveyed believe that SA Tourism could improve its performance in executing its mandate[1]. Stakeholders are widely sceptical about the veracity of the data that comes out of Statistics South Africa which forms the basis for SA Tourism's own analysis of international tourist arrivals. New data sources must be found to create a completer picture of international arrivals to South Africa, one that is both in line with global definitions, and meaningful to industry." The report also acknowledges that the new immigration regulations is "of concern."

A full list of recommendations is provided in Annexure A of the Report. Below is a brief simmary of some of the key recommendations:

The Role and Mandate of South African Tourism
- Greater collaboration with the private sector to increase South Africa's global tourism market share.
- A new institutional home for the Tourism Grading Council of South Africa.
- Review of certain aspects of SA Tourism's organisational development and design, including the country office model, to enhance effective delivery of the marketing mandate.

International Marketing
- Handing over the management of Indaba to an independent operator, given that industry is now actively and successfully operating in this space (as evidenced by WTM Africa), and the

drain that Indaba places on SA Tourism resources.
- Review its practices for buyer selection and participation at international tourism shows (particularly of provinces and cities, and its own large travel delegations).

Domestic Tourism
- Address fragmentation by applying one brand strategy across international and domestic markets.
- Launch a new 'tourism nation' campaign, particularly post-xenophobia attacks. The Welcome campaign is an example of such a campaign.

South African National Convention Bureau (SANCB)
- Improve research and analysis for business tourism, including data from business events attendees (SANCB is in a position to get significant data through surveys of attendees at events).
- Maximise linkages between business and leisure tourism. Within the various strategies, plans, and research, there is no indication that this area has received any attention.

Institutional positioning and partnerships
- SA Tourism needs to work in a way that is fundamentally collaborative, where collaboration is a value and measure for the organisation.
- The role and function of the TBCSA as an overarching voice for the private sector of tourism is also mentioned.

Budget and Finance
- Provide NDT and National Treasury with a much clearer business case for investment in marketing, and consistently make the economic argument for budget allocations.
- Develop a clear strategy to improve collection of the TOMSA levy which includes demonstrating value for money.

Governance, Performance Management and Monitoring
- The Board of SA Tourism should co-opt additional specialist tourism marketing skills through subcommittees and ad hoc advisory committees to advise the Board on particular issues.
- An annual performance review should be conducted of the Board and its committees, including the extent to which it members contribute to its effectiveness.
- Organisational and Executive performance management reviews must be based on objective measures, and made public.

In conclusion, Minister Hanekom said a fully optimised SA Tourism is essential for the transformation and sustainable growth of the sector, and for tourism to achieve the National Development Goal target of creating 225 000 jobs by 2020. **it**

[1]Stakeholders' views are reported on extensively on this report. The Committee Panel does not necessarily agree with the views expressed.

Skills Development Levy Refund

Did you know that you can get a portion of your Skills Development Levy (SDL) back each year? **Charmaine Pratt** explains how.

What is SDL? SDL is a levy imposed by the South African Revenue Services (SARS) to encourage learning and development and is determined by an employer's salary bill. Every month, employers handover 1% of total salaries to SARS along with PAYE.

Who pays SDL? An employer whose total salary bill will exceed R500 000 over the next 12 months, becomes liable to pay SDL.

If you pay SDL there are various ways in which you can claim this money back. If you don't claim annually you lose it and the ability to reduce your overall training spend.

The Mandatory Grant claim allows you to claim back up to 20% of this levy from your industry SETA (CATHSSETA for the Tourism Industry) by meeting all the SETA requirements. Some of these requirement include submitting a workplace skills plan (WSP) and an Annual Training Report (ART). These are often daunting and companies generally get the help of a consultant but you will need to weigh up the cost of the consultant versus the potential claim before you proceed.

Employers can also apply for a discretionary grant which are funds that your SETA will give to you "at their discretion". At present 80% of the SETA discretionary funds will be used for Pivotal training. Pivotal stands for professional, vocational, technical and academic learning programmes that lead to a qualification on the National Qualifications Framework. So you can use this to upskill your team and even as a benefit to attract better staff.

Other discretionary funding available is bursaries and internships. SETA's will support learners who have been accepted to study at any South African Public Institution by offering learners bursaries to further their studies. The bursary grant can be used to pay study fees, textbooks, accommodation, meals and other related costs depending on the funding policy of the SETA.

Internships are structured work based programmes designed to give unemployed graduates exposure to work experience. Many SETA's offer internships based on set criteria. Monthly stipend payments are funded through the SETA for the duration of the internship programme.

Most companies don't even know that this comes off their payroll and is paid to SARS let alone that they can structure their training programs to claim back the maximum benefit.

Should you need assistance with assessing your ability to claim for grants, contact Charmaine at Sprout Consulting via email to *charmaine@sproutconsulting.co.za*. **it**

if this is your idea of a training budget...
...we need to talk!

Did you know that you can get a portion of your Skills Development Levy (SDL) back this year?
Contact Sprout Consulting to find out how!

- Claim back up to 20% of this levy from the Tourism Industry SETA (CATHSSETA)
- We can help in submitting a Workplace Skills Plan and an Annual Training Report
- Apply for a discretionary grant for Pivotal training, bursaries and internships
- Structure training programs to claim back the maximum benefit

HR | MARKETING | ACCOUNTING | IT

sprout CONSULTING
your outsourced head office

info@sproutconsulting.co.za | **www.sproutconsulting.co.za** [f]

Tour Operators:
10 Tips for Embracing Change

Finding your way when changing office procedures.

In this first part of an ongoing series of articles on office automation for Tour Operators, **Linday de Heer** provides useful advice and tips to help find your way when changing office procedures.

"Change is the heartbeat of Growth" (Scottie Somers) – resisting change can inhibit possibilities.

There are many phases to the change process, and each step needs to be embraced to bring about the positivity your efforts deserve. Hanging on to the comfort zone of your surroundings can erode your goals; what you set out to achieve at the beginning of your dream can alter the perception of your company.

Finding your feet when establishing an office process or system can be a challenge and often we make do with the seemingly simplest and affordable route. Smaller companies; even with a view to gradual growth can often be short sighted in their business processing needs; plugging holes and shortfalls with quick fixes that become the norm.

What often makes matters worse is when we are able to admit that our current system is inadequate but we simply cannot bring ourselves to embrace the change that is required to perfect the business processing system. This in itself has a negative effect on perspective growth as well as those we influence around us.

It is also important to see how being held ransom by those who are not decision makers, but influencers can have a dramatic effect on your growth. Be aware of those who refuse to be a part of necessary change; they may not have the same vision as you, and in this way inhibit your achievements.

We all endeavour to put our best foot forward. In the competitive world of Tourism where the slightest differences between your company and the company next door can have a huge impact on your business; ask yourself, why would you risk that, why not be a market leader and re order, restructure and embrace the change that secures your future.

10 Tips to Embracing Change for Tour Operators:

01 **Discuss the plan with your consultants**.

Let them see the benefit. Making a management decision without consultant buy-in can result in implementation failure.

02 **Make sure your consultants are properly trained**.

Comprehensive training is vital for the successful implementation of any new product. Without adequate training the consultants will be left feeling frustrated and will struggle with the new process.

03 **Management also need training!**

To understand all requirements, and to have realistic expectations of the system on your consultants, at least one member of the management team should become an expert on this system.

04 **Be strong!**

Management should always set a deadline of when the new system will be used in the office. Once planning, implementation and training have taken place, set a date and stick to it – this ensures that consultants don't slip back in to their outdated work habits.

05 **Offer an incentive.**

Consultants will respond to making a little more commission for all bookings made, within a certain period, on the new system.

06 **Manage expectations.**

Don't expect things to work 100% overnight. Change takes time and needs to be managed and adapted to work for your office environment.

A SOFTWARE PACKAGE DESIGNED **FOR TOUR OPERATORS**

TRAVELOGIC™
Tour Operator Software

Automate your Workflow through Technology.

Produce Fast and Accurate Quotations.

Management Reports, Itineraries and Invoices.

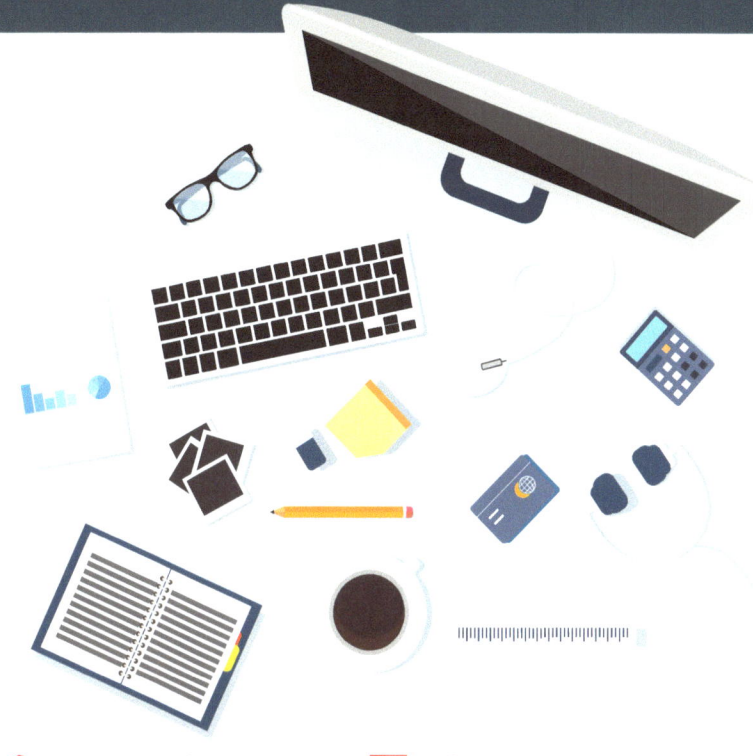

Remote Access and Live 3rd Party Availability.

🔗 www.travelogic.co.za   ✉ info@travelogic.co.za

10 Tips to Embracing Change for Tour Operators:

07 **Preparation is key.**

The more prepared and organised you are the better.

08 **Be adaptable.**

Be prepared to change other office procedures in order to implement a new one. See this as a positive way to improve upon current procedure.

09 **Communicate with your provider.**

Make sure that they understand your needs, and any challenges you may be having, so that they have the opportunity to assist before you become too frustrated.

10 **Change is good.**

Embrace it and enjoy the benefits!

Mind shift

Letting go of your existing office workflow processes, is a bit like having someone else pack your kitchen cupboards. That feeling of not having control, not being able to find anything and trying many doors before finding what you are looking for can be daunting.

But what if the reordering of your kitchen actually meant that you spent less time there? What if it improved your workflow and you spent less time going back and forth between your appliances? What if you enjoyed your new space so much, that it inspired you to be more creative and productive?

How does this analogy translate to tour operator software? Simple. Tour operator software can reorganise your workflow, ensuring that you save time, improve accuracy and eliminate any unnecessary processes.

A purpose designed tour operator software solution looks at the core principles of your business requirements; • Fast • Accurate • Efficient • User Friendly • Client facing documentation • Reporting functionality.

So if there are so many benefits to moving to a software solution, why is the change still so daunting? Well, let's go back to the kitchen analogy again; if you take time to open each cupboard, see how things have been repacked, move between each appliance, and locate your most importance utensils, you are already 90% of the way to becoming aware of your new space.

Still afraid to take the plunge?

That's okay; Travelogic have done this before, and are on hand to offer advice and guidance through the implementation process. Their experienced management team and skilled developers are here to ensure that your move from a manual to a software solution is as smooth and stress-free as possible.   i₹

─────────── READ MORE ───────────

Online at 'How to keep itineraries current' or in the March 2015 edition of the Tourism Tattler Trade Journal (pages 11-13) and 'How to streamline your Tour Operator business' in the May 2015 edition (page 14).

About the author: Lindsay de Heer is the Managing Director of Equilogic (Pty) Ltd - a South African software company that specialises in Tour Operator management automation. For more information visit www.travelogic.co.za

Competition

'Like' / 'Share' / 'Connect' with these Social Media icons to win!

The winning 'Like' or 'Share' during the month of **August 2015** will receive a
Picnic Blanket in a bag with the compliments of
Livingstones Supply Co – *Suppliers of the Finest Products to the Hospitality Industry*.

Livingston Supply Company

Tourism Tattler

August Prize: A Fully Lined Picnic Blanket

The Picnic Blanket in a bag is 1.5m x 1.5m in size. Available in Kikoy, Shwe Shwe and African fabrics, and fully lined with waterproofing on the one side.

Win

Competition Rules: Only one winner will be selected each month on a random selection draw basis. The prize winner will be notified via social media. The prize will be delivered by the sponsor to the winners postal address within South Africa. Should the winner reside outside of South Africa, delivery charges may be applicable. The prize may not be exchanged for cash.

Congratulations to our Social Media winner for July 2015

Winner

Tsitsikamma Village Inn has been selected as our **July 2015** winner for their @TsitsikammaVI 'follow' on **Twitter**. Tsitsikamma Village Inn will receive a **Candola Papilio Lantern** with the compliments of **Livingstones Supply Co** – *Suppliers of the Finest Products to the Hospitality Industry.*

About Tsitsikamma Village Inn: The historic Tsitsikamma Village Inn, was established in 1946. This hotel is situated in the Storms River Village tucked away in the lush Tsitsikamma forest, close to Storms River Mouth, in the Tsitsikamma National Park. This historic South African hotel has served as a stop-over for travellers for more than a century. Most of the rooms are situated around a typical Village green.

These buildings reflect many of the different building styles t hat were to be found in the Cape Colony during the 1800s.

For more information visit
www.tsitsikammavillageinn.co.za
or connect on twitter.com/TsitsikammaVI

About the Prize from Livingstones Supply Co::

Candola products are based on a simple, but unusually functional principle which guarantees many practical advantages for restaurants and hotels in the everyday application. Instead of conventional candles, Candola uses a bottle, which is filled with a special totally odourless mineral oil.

The wick soaks up the mineral oil from the container and delivers a candle light without smoke and soot. Thus, there is no melted wax as with candles - and consequently no wax residue. Right to the very last drop of oil, the lamp looks as if it was being used for the very first time

Another advantage for restaurants. The oil bottle is hidden under a decorative sleeve. This also guarantees a positive safety side effect. When the lamp tips over the flame goes out immediately. However, apart from these purely functional aspects, the success of Candola is based on the product development.

For more information visit www.livingstonessupplyco.co.za

WYSTC 2015
CAPE TOWN
22-25 SEPTEMBER • SOUTH AFRICA

The essential global youth travel industry event

REGISTER NOW

GROW YOUR BUSINESS
IN THE GLOBAL YOUTH TRAVEL INDUSTRY

Now in its 24th year, the World Youth and Student Travel Conference - WYSTC 2015 - is the must-attend business-to-business trade conference for key stakeholders and organisations working in youth, student and educational travel.

It's the first time that WYSTC will be held on the African continent and we won't be back for a while, so don't miss the opportunity to meet with **over 600 industry professionals** representing more than **450 organisations** across **120 countries** at the Cape Town International Convention Centre this September.

Register now at www.wystc.org

Tap in to the thriving youth travel industry

Gain the latest insights

Take part in pre-scheduled business appointments

JOIN WYSE TRAVEL CONFEDERATION AND SAVE!

Our members **save EUR 600 per delegate** on WYSTC 2015 registration.

You will also benefit from being part of the world's largest and most powerful network of youth, student and educational travel operators, which serves **over 30 million** young travellers each year.

Visit **www.wysetc.org** for more information and to join.

- Comprehensive seminar and workshop programme
- Meet hosted buyers from across the globe
- Sponsorship and exhibitor packages
- Global Youth Travel Awards
- Networking events

 /wystc   **@WYSTC | #WYSTC2015**   **www.wystc.org**

WYSTC is the annual event of 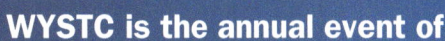  **WYSE TRAVEL CONFEDERATION**

2015 Rhino Conservation Awards

PRINCE ALBERT II OF MONACO FOUNDATION

The heroic actions of those that fight for the conservation of rhino were recently acknowledged, celebrated and rewarded at the 2015 Rhino Conservation Awards, writes **Andrew Campbell** of the Game Ranger's Association of Africa.

Dr Hansen and Dr Kaschke handing over the Patron Award to HSH Prince Albert II of Monaco.

At the gala-dinner ceremony, held on 27 July at the Montecasino Ballroom, the patron of the Awards, HSH Prince Albert II of Monaco delivered the keynote address, and congratulated the winners for their exemplary efforts.

The winner in the **Best Field Ranger** category was **Patrick Mwita**. With intense knowledge of the black rhino population in the Southern Serengeti, Patrick effectively monitors the animals and has also bravely averted armed poaching attempts. The first and second runners up in this category were **William Ndobe** (*local legend in the Kruger National Park [KNP] with 31 years of service*) and **Jeoffrey Kubayi** (*KNP field ranger, dog handler, tracker and poaching incursion detector*).

Winners of the Special Youth category, Alyssa Carter; Calvin Erasmus; Kirsten Everett; and Kelsey Hunt.

Black Mamba APU won the **Best Conservation Practitioner** category. This Anti-Poaching Unit, which consists of 26 women, conducts anti-poaching operations and focuses on educating the communities surrounding the Balule Nature Reserve in the benefits of conservation and rhino protection. Runners up were **Don English** (*in charge of general conservation as well as rhino protection in the KNP's region with the highest density of rhino*) and **Bruce Leslie** (*Regional Ranger Special Operations, revolutionising tactical rhino anti-poaching operations in the KNP*).

Taking the win in the **Best Political and Judicial Support** category was **His Majesty King Mswati III**, the King of Swaziland who has played a pivotal role in the protection of wildlife and, especially, rhino. Second place was awarded to both **Adv Isabet Erwee** (*national record for the highest sentence ever handed down in a rhino poaching matter*) and **Adv Ansie Venter** (*one of the Specialised Prosecutors, Organised Crime, Mpumalanga*). Third place was awarded to **Mario Scholtz** (*responsible for the investigation of rhino poaching related aspects in SANParks*).

The winner of the **Best Science, Research and Technology** category was **Dr Jacques Flamand**, who heads up the **Black Rhino Range Expansion Project**. Runners up were **Dr Johan Marais** (*for surgery on poached rhino*) and **Piet Beytell** (*Principle Conservation Scientist for MET, Namibia*).

Elise Daffue of StopRhinoPoaching.com won the award for **Best Awareness, Education or Funding**. Second and third place went to **Unite Against Poaching** (*a Unitrans Volkswagen fundraising initiative*) and the Peace Parks Foundation). it

Rhino Poaching Deaths vs Poacher Arrests - Stats for South Africa by Province

Year	2010		2011		2012		2013		2014		2015	
Deaths vs Arrests	Deaths	Arrests	Deaths	Arrests	Deaths	Arrests	Deaths	Arrests	Deaths	Arrests	Deaths	Arrests
KNP (SanParks)	146	67	252	82	425	73	606	133	827	174	29	09
MNP (SanParks)	00	00	06	00	03	00	03	00	00	00	00	00
MAP (SanParks)	00	00	00	00	00	00	00	00	01	01	00	00
Gauteng	15	10	03	16	01	26	08	10	05	21	00	00
Limpopo	52	36	80	34	59	43	114	34	110	60	12	00
Mpumalanga	17	16	31	73	28	66	92	00	83	45	02	04
North West	57	02	31	21	77	32	87	70	65	14	00	03
Eastern Cape	04	07	11	02	07	00	05	26	15	02	00	00
Free State	03	00	04	00	00	06	04	07	04	00	00	00
KwaZulu-Natal	38	25	34	04	66	20	85	63	99	68	06	01
Western Cape	00	02	06	00	02	00	00	00	01	01	00	00
Northern Cape	01	00	00	00	00	01	00	00	05	00	00	00
TOTAL	**333**	**165**	**448**	**232**	**668**	**267**	**1004**	**343**	**1215**	**386**	**49**	**17**

KNP = Kruger National Park, MNP = Mpumalanga National Park, MAP = Mapungubwe National Park. Statistics released by the DEAT as at 22 January 2015.

Incidents of poaching can be reported to the anonymous tip-off lines 0800 205 005, 08600 10111 or Crime-Line on 32211.

In loving memory of "Cecil"

Dedicated to creating an Africa where communities and wildlife live together in harmony

Founded in 2013, the SATIB Conservation Trust (SCT) seeks to find solutions and fund approved wildlife research projects, anti-poaching programmes and community education initiatives that deliver tangible and sustainable results to reduce conflict between the human and animal inhabitants of Africa, ultimately ensuring the conservation of the continent's wildlife.

Elephants Alive, Elephants for Africa, Hwange Lion Research Project, Lion Management Forum of South Africa, the Kgalagadi National Park Lion research project, the Rhino Youth Summit and the Niassa National Park anti-poaching and aerial surveillance initiatives are some of the projects that the SCT supports and assists with both financially and

materially. The recent hunting of the research Lion "Cecil" on the fringes of the Hwange National Park in Zimbabwe, has highlighted the need for support of various conservation projects via established and recognised organisations like the SCT. Research, welfare and conservation bodies need constant help in the on-going struggle against adverse conditions, essential running expenses and outside pressures from illegal hunting, poaching and local communities, all of which hamper the survival of animals whose populations are in decline.

Please help the SATIB Conservation Trust in their quest to continue the good work they are doing by donating! Details can be found on our website: www.satibtrust.com

For more information about the SATIB Conservation Trust, please contact Brian Courtenay:
E bcourtenay@satibtrust.com | C +27 (0)82 926 0791 | T +27 (0)31 514 4200

www.satibtrust.com

SATIB CONSERVATION TRUST
WILDLIFE & COMMUNITIES

SATIB Conservation Trust is a registered Public Benefit Organization with SARS (Registered Trust IT 18/2012PMB; PBO 930039588)

Sports & Events Tourism Exchange

27 - 29 October 2015
Protea Hotel Fire & Ice! Menlyn, Tshwane

SAVE THE DATE

NEW CITY

NEW FORMAT

NEW FOCUS

A B2B platform aimed at positioning South Africa as a Sports and Events Tourism Destination.

The annual Sports and Events Tourism Exchange, now in its fifth year, is the only event of its kind in Southern Africa and provides a platform that brings together businesses from the sports, events and tourism industries, SETE encourages collaboration between these sectors over a two-day conference, two-day table top exhibition and networking events.

Sports & Events Tourism Exchange (SETE) will see new and exciting changes including the change of the exhibition format. SETE has launched the Invitation-Only Table Top Exhibit this year which will be more affordable and efficient for focusing on important Buyer & Exhibitor Meetings and concluding business deals.

SETE 2015 will also be focusing on Golf Tourism as one of the key Sports Tourism Industries and will be targeting 10 - 15 International Golf Buyers.

The International Hosted Buyer Programme will again welcome pre-selected high calibre buyers to visit South Africa and interact with exhibiting companies at SETE. 30 buyers from the international sports and events tourism industries will be targeted as well as specific golf tourism buyers.

For more information contact:
Rene Staack
Rene@ThebeReed.co.za
+27 (0) 11 549 8300

www.sportsandevents.co.za

Organised by:

Host City Partner:

 /SETE.ZA

 @SETE_ZA

Meet the world

2 - 5 November 2015 / ExCel London

WTM® Buyers' Club

› **£2.5 billion*** of new business **generated at World Travel Market 2014** › WTM Speed **Networking** sessions attract more than 1,000 exhibitors › Meet up to **5,000**** exhibitors from across the world**

Exclusive benefits include:

fast track entry, private meeting rooms, dedicated lounges, complimentary refreshments, travel & entertainment discounts.

Find out more
wtmlondon.com/buyersclub

Official Media Partner
tourism TATTLER

Official Premier Partner
MÉXICO LIVE IT TO BELIEVE IT

2 - 5 November 2015 • London

* Source: Independent research by Fusion Communications, January 2015

**ABC audited figures, February 2015

World Travel Market and WTM are trademarks of Reed Elsevier Properties SA, used under license.

Three Industries: One Event

The annual Sports and Events Tourism Exchange (SETE), now in its fifth year, is the only event of its kind in Southern Africa and provides a platform that brings together businesses from the Sports, Events and Tourism industries, writes **Jacques Maritz**.

SETE encourages collaboration between these sectors over a two-day conference, two-day table top exhibition and includes multiple networking events, from 27 – 29 October 2015. The City of Tshwane will be the new host city partner for Sports & Events Tourism Exchange and the venue will be at the Protea Hotel Fire and Ice! Menlyn.

Over the past four years delegates attending the SETE conference benefited from international and local experts sharing their knowledge and expertise on contemporary issues affecting the events tourism industry. A key milestone achieved at last year's conference was agreement by the Sports & Events and Tourism industries, to support City of Durban's bid for the 2022 Commonwealth Games.

The new conference format involves a series of panel discussions with key stakeholders affected by each topic. An expert will facilitate each session providing high level trends of each topic and the key issues that should be debated.

Delegates representing senior decision-makers from the sports, events and tourism sectors mainly from South Africa and consisting of government officials and members of the private sector will be in attendance. Academics, NGOs and community stakeholders will also be represented.

A key focus this year will be on promoting South Africa as a Golf Tourism Destination and other topics that will feature on the programme will include:
1. Promoting South Africa's Golf Tourism Products;
2. Commercial Viability of Golf Estates using International Case Studies;
3. Success of Major Golf Events to Promote Destinations;
4. The Importance of School Sport and the Linkages to Growing Domestic Tourism;
5. Lessons from Commonwealth Games Host Destinations in the Management of the Games;
6. The Use of Technology for the Development of High Performance Athletes;
7. Commercial Viability and Sustainability of Event Venues;
8. Marketing Trends of Events using Case Studies of Major Events.

The organizers, Thebe Reed Exhibitions has launched the "Invitation - Only Table Top Exhibits" this year, which will be more affordable and efficient for focusing on important Buyer & Exhibitor Meetings and concluding business deals.

The City Manager of Tshwane, Jason Ngobeni said: "As part of the Tshwane Vision 2055 the Sports & Events Tourism Exchange fits perfectly into our objective, to ensure that Tshwane can be positioned as a premier events destination. Growing the local economy that is inclusive, diversified, and competitive. During the Tshwane Open, the City of Tshwane presented golf enthusiasts with high-calibre national and international golfers who competed for world ranking. Co-sanctioned by the European Tour and Sunshine Tour, and one of the six founding professional golf tours that make up the International Federation of PGA Tours, ties into one of SETE's main themes this year - that of Golf Tourism".

"We welcome the City of Tshwane as Host City partner for the fifth edition of the annual SETE event. Over the past few years Tshwane has hosted numerous major events and there is no doubt that SETE will contribute to the City's objective of being recognized as the country's premier events destination. We look forward to this partnership and thank the City for having the vision to invest in this event" concluded Commercial Director, Thebe Reed Exhibitions, Sugen Pillay.

To book your attendance for Sports and Events Tourism Exchange 2015 contact Rene Staack on rene@thebereed.co.za or call +27(0)11 549 8300. it

For more information visit www.sportsandevents.co.za

About the Author: Jacques Maritz is the Media Liaison for SETE and can be contacted on +27 (0)84 444 0775 or via email at Jmps@worldonline.co.za.

About Thebe Reed Exhibitions: Operated as a joint venture between Thebe Tourism Group Pty Limited and Reed Exhibitions, Thebe Reed Exhibitions is Southern Africa's most forward thinking and successful exhibition and venue management company responsible for exhibitions such as the Africa Travel Week consisting of ILTM Africa, IBTM Africa and WTM® Africa; the Business Entrepreneurship and Franchise Expo; Decorex SA; 100% Design South Africa; the Gauteng Motor Fest; Mediatech Africa and the Sports & Events Tourism Exchange (SETE). Thebe Reed Exhibitions aims to provide the best platform for showcasing industries and nurturing business and networking opportunities on the African continent. For more information visit www.ThebeReed.co.za

Your service may be up to scratch...

...but is your minimum wage?

South Africa's Hospitality Sector minimum wage has been adjusted with effect from 1 July 2015. The change in the minimum wage is in line with the Basic Conditions of Employment Act (BCEA) which empowers Labour Minister, Mildred Oliphant to adjust wages in the sector. The new minimum wage will be applicable until 30 June 2016.

HOSPITALITY SECTOR MINIMUM WAGES - 1 JULY 2015 to 30 June 2016

Minimum wages for employers with 10 or less employees			Minimum wages for employers with more than 10 employees		
Monthly	Weekly	Daily	Monthly	Weekly	Daily
R2 760.59	R637.10	R14.15	R3 076.98	R710.12	R15.77

Please note: The current wage increases have been determined by utilizing the CPI. The current level of CPI is 4.6%. The minimum wage increases is therefore determined by adding 4.6% plus 1.5% as stated in the current Sectoral Determination. The total increase is 6.1%. For more information on the media statement from the minister, please go to. *http://www.labour.gov.za/DOL/media-desk/media-statements/2015/hospitality-sector-has-a-new-minimum-wage* Should you have any queries or need assistance with Payroll Processing and Structuring, please contact Charmaine Pratt.

Sprout Consulting is proud to be associated with the following businesses in the Hospitality Sector.

HR | MARKETING | ACCOUNTING | IT

info@sproutconsulting.co.za | *www.sproutconsulting.co.za*

your outsourced head office

Property Profile

mantis
Hotels, Eco-Escapes & Lifestyle Resorts

BUSH LODGE
Amakhala
GAME RESERVE

As Mantis strives to offer travellers the most exceptional properties and authentic experiences imaginable, the company is proud to introduce Bush Lodge on 'Amakhala Game Reserve, who join Oceana Beach & Wildlife Reserve and Plettenberg Park in the Mantis Eastern Cape collection.

Mantis is a family run collection of award winning, privately owned, 5-star properties located around the World, across all seven continents. Its specialist areas include Boutique Hotels, Game Reserves, Eco Lodges, Ski Lodges, Chalets and Boutique Cruises, offering in-the-know travellers the most exceptional properties and authentic experiences imaginable.

Each of the diverse, handpicked properties represents the finest example of its kind and celebrates the culture, gastronomy, architecture and nature of the locations in which they are found. Whilst every property is unique, being part of the collection ensures that the quality of the facilities, service and overall experience is consistently 5-star and guests can always expect personal, friendly service.

Officially founded by entrepreneur and hotelier Adrian Gardiner in 2000, Mantis is committed to the spirit of conservation and restoration, and each property is sensitive to its surroundings in respect of the building, environment and local community. The entrepreneurial spirit of the family underpins that of the group, allowing them to be dynamic in the growth of the portfolio, and to respond quickly to consumer demand.

In 2013, Mantis launched Mantis eXtreme, which offers an online collection of authentic, once-in-a-lifetime encounters and experiences worldwide, often paired with product from their field of expertise - five star, handpicked properties. Experiences include: Wilderness camps in the great Niassa at Lugenda Wilderness Camp, Mozambique; Bear Grylls Survival Academy, U.K., USA, Africa; Parabolic flights with Space Affairs, Europe; Rhino Encounters with Dr. Will Fowlds, South Africa; Midnight Golf, Bjorkliden, Sweden and Great Bear Tours, Canada.

Mantis and Mantis eXtreme offer member properties the ideal sales, marketing and management solution for their boutique business to ensure successful growth and drive long term brand development. The company also offers consultancy services in other disciplines including conservation, education and hotel development.

Bush Lodge is a 5-star Game Lodge nestled in the bush at the top of the vast open valley on the Amakhala Game Reserve. This lodge offers en-suite; tented and thatched suits. The open plan design of the tents invites the cooling breeze closer over the water, transporting all the authentic African sounds, tastes and smells right onto your doorstep. Each unit features a private outdoor shower with magnificent views through the unit towards your own glimpse of the water hole. A personal deck allows you to get lost in Africa while spoiling yourself with elite conveniences, such as opulent furniture and all the creature comforts you would expect from the best tented camps in the world.

Guests can enjoy all-inclusive meals in the dining area and relax in the shared lounge or by the outdoor fireplace. In addition to game drives and bush walks, there is also the opportunity for bird watching.

Bush Lodge is located 50 km from Addo Elephant Park and 47 km from Grahamstown. Port Elizabeth Airport is 100 km away.

Graded 4-Star by the TGCSA, the facilities at Bush Lodge include: laundry service, indoor fireplace, braai/barbecue, air conditioning, swimming pool, and outdoor terrace. Credit card facilities are available, and WiFi in public areas is free of charge.

The Amakhala Game Reserve is approximately 7000ha in size. To reduce human impact and maintain exclusivity, the number of guests allowed on the reserve at any one time is set by a self imposed limitation of the number of guests to the hectares of the reserve, one bed per 50ha.

For more information visit www.mantiscollection.com/property/bush-lodge/

Oceana Beach and Wildlife Reserve is a luxurious haven in South Africa's Eastern Cape, and the only combined ocean and game reserve in Southern Africa. The resort forms part of Mantis Collection's ultimate Garden Route journey. A short drive from the quaint seaside town of Port Alfred and with a seven kilometre stretch of private soft sandy beach on one side and 850 hectares of unspoilt bush on the other, this really is the best of both worlds.

Friendly faces and delicious fruit cocktails await your arrival at Oceana. While your luggage is taken to your suite fall into one of the comfy couches in the lounge, browse the books in the library or take a walk to the games room where you'll find, among other things, a pool table and organic tea, coffee and hot chocolate for you to help yourself at any time. Each of the Lodge Suites have been decorated in the theme of the different animals you may encounter while there. Inspired by local artefacts, the décor is authentic to the surroundings

The opulent Private Ocean House can accommodate up to six people and is decorated in an understated African chic style. With every luxury catered for, no stone has been left unturned. From private dinners and long soaks in the heated Jacuzzi, it's an entertainer's dream without the cleaning up. The Oceana Wellness Centre overlooking the infinity rock pool has two treatment rooms with heated beds and the double treatment room has a soothing jet bath. After a three course lunch feast you might feel like a workout in the well-equipped gym or simply relax and let the toxins seep away in the spacious steam room.

For more information: www.mantiscollection.com/property/oceana-beach-wildlife-reserve/

Plettenberg Park Hotel & Spa is poised in exquisite beauty on the Robberg Peninsula in Plettenberg Bay. Here guests can escape to a natural paradise where time stands still as nature unfolds.

The hotel is situated in a private nature reserve, nestling on a cliffs edge, offering guests dramatically sweeping views of the Indian Ocean. The accent is on uniqueness, time honoured values, excellent personal service and superb cuisine. It is a perfect location for today's discerning traveler who seeks something both benefiting and inspiring to one's inner well being.

Plettenberg Park has been a host to many distinguished guests, such as Nelson Mandela and Richard Branson amongst many others who have visited Plettenberg bay.

Each room has a private balcony to allow guests to enjoy the view. Rooms contain large sleigh beds (single and double) with ample cupboard space, under floor heating, flat screen TV, DVD player, in room safe, gowns and slippers, and in room magazines. There is a mini bar with a full range of snacks and beverages.

The ten rooms are comprised of:
4 x Large Luxury Rooms,
4 x Large Luxury Twin Rooms, and
2 x Small Luxury Twin Rooms.
Plettenberg Park will arrange all activities and excursions for guests, from whale or bird watching, to nature walks, fishing, snorkeling, scuba diving, horse riding or golf.

Visit: www.mantiscollection.com/property/plettenberg-park-hotel-spa-south-africa/

Anyone can save a life.
All it takes is a donation.

Sea Rescue

Advertisement sponsored courtesy of Ogilvy & Mather / Tourism Tattler as a service to the travel trade.

Restaurant Review

Waffling on about Waffles

My misconception of waffles being a mere base for sweet desserts has been dispelled since visiting the Waffle House in Ramsgate, South Africa, writes
Des Langkilde

Waffle: (noun) *'A light crisp cake made of batter and baked in a waffle iron'*. As a verb, the word means; *'To be unable to make a decision'*, which at The Waffle House is an appropriate analogy, as the ubiquitous waffle forms the base of a wide and varied menu that leaves patrons in a state of mouth watering indecision.

From sweet to savoury, carnivorous to vegetarian, banting to wholesome free-range toppings - all available with a gluten-free waffle base option - the menu caters to all tastes and dietary preferences.

But The Waffle House is not just about good food - the ambiance created by the venues location alongside a small stream, with a picturesque foot bridge leading into indigenous forest pathways bordering the Ramsgate Lagoon and leading to the beach, adds to its attraction. The venue is also wheelchair friendly, has free WiFi and a children's play area.

Visitors looking for mementos or gifts to take back home will find the Gaze Gallery and Basket Shop to be a treasure trove, with works by renown South African artists, potters and crafters on display.

Where it all began

Dating back to 1957, the birth of The Waffle House in Ramsgate, South Africa, heralded the beginning of an exciting journey for John and Doreen Gaze. Opening the restaurant of their dreams, known at that time as the Tea House of the Blue Lagoon, they had no idea it would become the famous South Coast tourism attraction that it is today. After a 15 year period during which John and Doreen leased out the premises, they took it back in 1991 and renamed it The Waffle House. This was in line with two Waffle House restaurants that their eldest son had opened in the UK. The first was in Norwich, Norfolk, which opened in 1978, and the second in St. Albans, Hertfordshire. Today, the Waffle House is one of the busiest restaurants on the South Coast, specialising in good food and good service, This 220 seater restaurant is popular amongst locals and visitors alike. Holiday seasons are particularly busy, however the well trained and friendly staff consistently rise to the challenge of producing and serving quality products throughout the year.

History of the Waffle

The modern waffle has its origins in Europe and was mentioned in poems of the late 12th century when they were made and sold on the streets, especially to celebrate feast days. In medieval Europe, vendors were permitted to sell their waffles outside churches on Saints' days and during other special religious celebrations. Competition at the churches eventually became very heated, and at times so violent, that King Charles IX of France imposed a regulation on waffle sales, requiring vendors to maintain a distance of at least *deux toises* (4 m/12 ft) from one another.

For more information, call +27 (0)39 314 9424 or go to www.wafflehouse.co.za or www.ramsgate.co.za

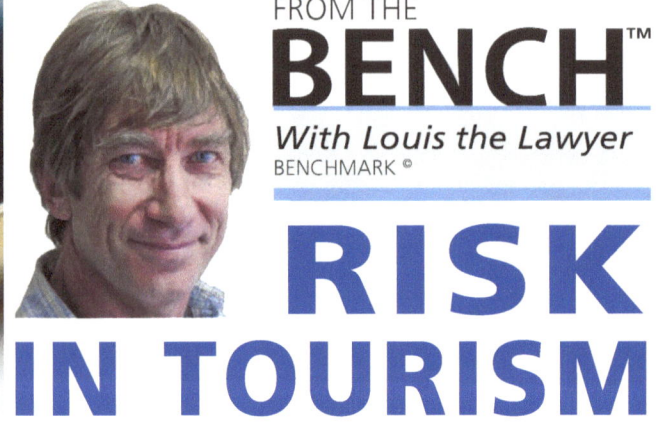

Legal

FROM THE BENCH™

With Louis the Lawyer
BENCHMARK ©

RISK IN TOURISM

– PART 13 –
THE LAW: CONTRACTS

Part 1 *(page 36 August 2014)*, categorised risk into five sections; **1. PEOPLE, 2. MONEY, 3. LAW, 4. SERVICE** and **5. ECOLOGY**.

Part 2, *(page 22 September 2014)*, covered **PEOPLE** under four sub-categories: **Staff** (discussed in Part 1); **Third party service providers ('TPSP')**; and **Business Associates**.

Part 3 *(page 24 October 2014)*, continued with **PEOPLE** as **Customers**.

Part 4 *(page 27 November 2014)*, started the discussion on **MONEY** in terms of CASH and CHEQUES.

Part 5 *(page 23 December 2014)*, covered CREDIT and CREDIT CARDS.

Part 6 *(page 25 January 2015)*, started the **LAW** category with CONTRACTS - an introduction and Requisite #1: Offer & Acceptance.

Part 7 *(page 18 February 2015)*, continued with Requisite #1 covering telephone enquiries, e-mails, websites and advertising.

Part 8 *(page 17 March 2015)*, covered Requisites #2: Legally Binding Obligation, and #3: Consensus in contracts.

Part 9 *(page 20 April 2015)*, covered Requisite #4: Performance Must Be Possible.

Part 10 *(page 31 May 2015)*, covered Requisites #5 & 6: Performance Must Be Permissible, and Capacity of the Contracting Parties.

Part 11 *(page 21 June 2015)*, continued with Requisite #6: Capacity of the Contracting Parties.

Part 12 *(page 23 July 2015)*, covered Requisite #7" Negotiating a Contract.

REQUISITE #8: DRAFTING A CONTRACT

As stated in previous articles, <u>an agreement does not have to be in writing</u> and <u>verbal agreements are perfectly binding</u>. However, we reduce such verbal agreements to writing because *'when the wheels come off'*, the *'finger pointing'* and *'who said what'* very quickly puts paid to the consensus you thought you had.

How do you go about reducing it to writing – can you do it yourself or do you have to speak to the legal fraternity? The answer to this is that you can indeed do it yourself to a large extent, but other than the factual issues (even that), it should be given to a lawyer to cast his eye over to ensure you have said the right thing, stated it correctly, and that it is binding from a legal perspective. However never ask a lawyer to *'have a quick look at your document'*: it implies that you want a cheap job, that what you've done should suffice and he merely has to rubber stamp it, and that his contribution is no more than a sop. It will put pressure on him to cut corners, whereas he is requested to put his professional reputation on the line – it is simply not fair to either party. As the saying goes *'If something is worth doing, it is worth doing it well'*.

It should be borne in mind that more often that not it is a good idea to involve your lawyer in the equation as early as possible, although this should be assessed on a case by case basis, depending on the complexity of the matter and the relationship you have with your lawyer (As you know, the relationship I aim to achieve with my clients via my **BASTA™ Legal Advice Clubs** is that of a *'legal GP'* thereby being part of your ongoing long term planning and strategy, ensuring the latter is legally sound permanently and not simply ad hoc). There is nothing worse (and more expensive) than 'dumping a pile of paper' on a lawyer's desk after weeks of meetings and then expecting him to produce an adequate agreement.

Why involve your lawyer in the 'build up to the final contract'?
He can steer the parties in a more effective direction and guide the thinking, strategy and the implementation. Such guidance will (or at least should) include taking cognizance of the facts and the law: this includes latest case law and statutes that may impact on the ultimate contract. He will furthermore be in a position to interpret such matters as body language and innuendos, things he simply can't pick up from the dreaded pile of paper. Such involvement on a proactive basis will also result in reduced legal fees: not only from

a time factor but also because a final draft will be produced at an earlier stage. Regardless of the option the parties implement, it is very important to spell out quite clearly and as early as possible *'Who is going to do what and by when'* (the 'w.w.w.').

This also has a bearing/depends on drafting style. Some lawyers like to draft long, verbose and complex agreements. My personal style s to keep it simple (including the language), have lots of definitions and addendums and have the parties themselves draft the 'commercial components' of the agreement.

The reasons for this approach are:

1. **Keep it simple:** pretty obvious – it means it is easier for everyone to understand it!

2. **Lots of definitions:**
   * it means everybody will apply their minds;
   * consensus is reached on the meaning of key issues;
   * it shortens the agreement.

3. **Addendums:** (this goes hand in hand with next point)
   * it means that if anything changes in the future you simply have to change the addendum or add a new one, sign and attach it to the agreement;
   * it often also means you don't have to involve the lawyers!

4. **Commercial components:**
   * this pertains to factual matters which by definition is the province of the parties;
   * it does (more often than not) require a legal mind to refine it;
   * it can be contained in addendums;
   * the (often) long hours refining this does not mean concomitant legal fees!

5. **Template:** Aim to prepare a document that can be used as a template in future.
   * It will also assist in the parties applying their minds.
   * It will save legal fees in future.

Bear in mind that ideally the above should be preceded by a letter of commitment ('LOC') (see earlier articles). **it**

Disclaimer: *This article is intended to provide a brief overview of legal matters pertaining to the travel and tourism industry and is not intended as legal advice. © Adv Louis Nel, 'Louis The Lawyer', August 2015.*

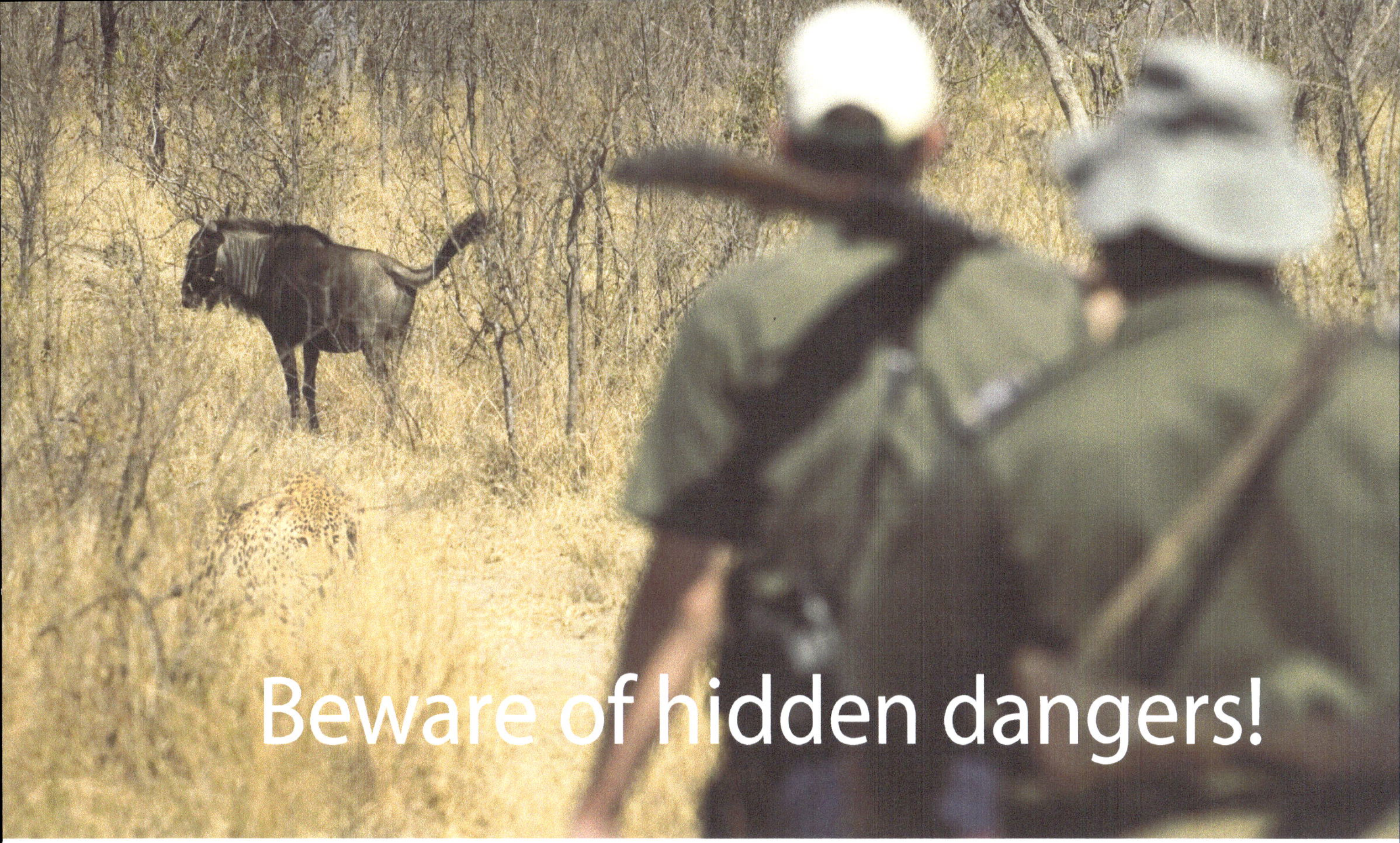

Beware of hidden dangers!

Introducing SATIB Professional Guides Insurance

It should come as no surprise that a career in the wild comes with various life threatening risks, leaving you vulnerable to serious injury, illness, disability and possibly death. Nature is unpredictable, no matter how many preventative measures are taken. There is just no guarantee against risks that can adversely affect you in such a dangerous environment. For those that run your own guiding business we know the ones who run the highest risk of all are the guests/clients under your care and supervision. With that kind of responsibility in your hands, you're going to need a comprehensive insurance policy, tailor made to suit the specific needs of your industry. SATIB Insurance Brokers is proud to offer a first in the South African Tourism Industry - A BRAND NEW Insurance Product for Professional Guides!

SATIB offer 4 possible insurance coverage plans to choose from, with monthly premiums that start as low as R188* per month. The plans themselves incorporate as much cover as is possible at this low premium spend and have been developed predominately for guides that do not currently have any insurance cover in place. The SATIB product is not meant to replace any existing medical aid or life cover but rather serves as a means to supplement your existing plans and add specific coverage that your existing policies just cannot offer you.

COVERS

- Accidental Death
- Permanent Disability
- Temporary, Partial or Total Disability
- Serious Illness Income Protection
- Business Risk Liability

In addition the Ultra Plan for employed guides also offers Personal Asset & Liability Cover.

BENEFITS

- Access your profile through our online portal
- Up to date information about your policy, claims procedures, transaction history
- Download insurance cover certificates
- Control of your insurance cover

* Cost is for members of FGASA or SATSA on the Employed Guides Premium Plan.

For more information, please contact us on:
T 0861 SATIB 4U (72842 48) | E info@satib.co.za
www.satibguides.co.za

Adventure Tourism Rankings

The 2015 ATDI Report shows that many countries are recognising and prioritising adventure tourism, by benchmarking resources and policy against 10 pillars to drive growth, writes **Des Langkilde**.

The fifth edition of the Adventure Tourism Development Index (ATDI), released in March 2015 by the Adventure Travel Trade Association, assesses adventure tourism potential for countries around the world.

The purpose of the ATDI is to facilitate adventure tourism policy and planning aimed at driving economic growth that is environmentally and culturally sustainable. It uses 10 pillars, drawing data from a range of sources, to gauge a country's readiness to compete in the adventure tourism sector.

The 10 pillars are:

1.   Sustainable Development Policy
2.   Safety and Security
3.   Health
4.   Natural Resources
5.   Cultural Resources
6.   Adventure Activity Resources
7.   Humanitarian
8.   Entrepreneurship
9.   Tourism Infrastructure, and
10. Image.

The ATDI can be helpful to governments considering an adventure tourism development strategy or strengthening an existing one. Tracking performance in the ten pillar areas provides a guideline for responsible development, helping to identify areas in need of more focus and attention.

The ATDI 2015 contains 28 Developed countries and 163 Developing/ Emerging countries. Countries are designated Developed (blue) or Developing (green) based on UN classifications.

While the report (downloadable at *www.adventureindex.travel/docs/ atdi_2015.pdf*) focuses on countries in the high ranking cluster, an interactive ranking map at *www.adventureindex.travel/2010-results- visual.htm* shows each country's rank. Scores do not however reflect a country's current popularity or market presence in adventure tourism.

Interactive Map

The interactive map groups countries into three clusters: High (Top Tier), Medium (Middle Tier) and Low (Bottom Tier). These groupings represent nations with similar scores and therefore a country's competitive set. The idea being that countries ranked 'Medium' or 'Low' should aim to move into the 'High' category.

So, how do African countries compare?

South Africa (ranked 38) is in the top tier, along with its neighbours Botswana (16) and Namibia (54), and North African countries Egypt (18), Tunisia (43) and Morocco (32). According to the map, these countries are on a equivalent level with most countries in Asia, such as China (51) and Russia (24) and in South America, such as Brazil (44) and Peru (22).

In the Middle tier, Zambia (ranked 65) is competitive with Mozambique (98), Madagascar (82), Tanzania (101), Kenya (88), Uganda (91), Ethiopia (107), Ghana (97), Senegal (76), Mali (108), Algeria (72), Malawi (95). These countries are comparable with India (85), Serbia (71) and Columbia (61).

The rest of Africa's countries are ranked in the Bottom Tier, with the exception of Western Sahara for which no data was available.

Trends

According to the 2013 Adventure Tourism Market Study:

*   The adventure travel market in North America, South America and Europe has experienced an average yearly size increase of 65% from 2009 to 2012.
*   The average spend on adventure trips *excluding airfare and gear) increased nearly 20% over the same period.
*   The top three factors affecting destination choice are natural beauty, activities and climate.
*   69% of adventure travellers reported online research as their preparation method.
*   The percentage of adventure travellers using Facebook has more than doubled between 2010 and 2013.

For information visit www.adventureindex.travel

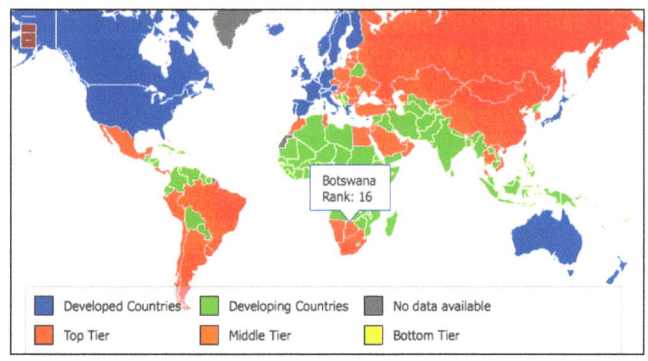

© Gravity Adventures/Dirty Boots

Think of us as your paddle...

SATIB are proud to launch a **newly designed** cover for Adventure Tourism operators that can be tailored to your specific needs and level of exposure. It is undoubtedly the most inclusive, yet flexible product on the market. So now when you get caught up the stream without a paddle, you know you're in safe hands.

Included is **SATIB24 Crisis Call**, Africa's leading critical incident management unit supported with an insurance component **ONLY** available to SATIB clients. They make the right decisions, ensuring best outcomes while reducing liability and your risk of reputational damage.

We deal with an average of 10 incidents daily - don't wait until it is too late - Call us **NOW**!

SATIB CONSERVATION TRUST
WILDLIFE & COMMUNITIES

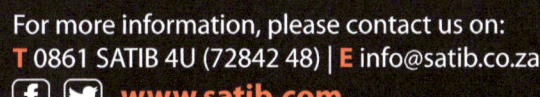

For more information, please contact us on:
T 0861 SATIB 4U (72842 48) | **E** info@satib.co.za

f 🐦 **www.satib.com**

SATIB
Insurance Brokers

SATIB Insurance Brokers Pty (Ltd) is an authorised Financial Services Provider. FSP License No. 16388/ IGF No. 002366. Compliance Officer: National Compliance CC Practice No 1307

Adventure Tourism Growth

The latest edition of UNWTO's 'Global Report on Adventure Tourism' cites Visa Facilitation as one of the most important areas to adventure tourism growth for destinations, writes **Des Langkilde**.

In the foreword to Volume nine of the UNWTO's 'Global Report on Adventure Tourism', the organisations Secretary General, Taleb Rifai describes adventure travel as a cornerstone of the tourism experience.

"For companies and destinations, adventure travel attracts visitors outside of peak season, highlights the natural and cultural values of a destination, thereby promoting its preservation, helps differentiate destinations against the competition, and creates resilient and committed travellers. These are just some of the reasons why it is fundamental for destinations to understand and work with adventure travel professionals," says Rifai.

The Report offers a thorough insightful analysis of the current and future adventure travel sector, providing global trends and structural knowledge on a significant, growing market, which is rapidly expanding..

"The Report highlights the importance of public-private sector collaboration initiatives within the adventure tourism sector. In a sector that is not only innovative, it is resilient in reaping the benefits that adventure tourism can bring to an economy, it is necessary to put in place conditions that make the country easy to visit as well as attractive to develop," says Yolanda Perdomo, Director of the UNWTO Affiliate Members Programme.

The 88 page report covers a broad range of subject matter in eight chapters, from an introduction with types of adventure tourism, to trends, structure, and potential benefits to local economies, communities and the environment. Chapters five through to eight deal with creating the right environment for adventure tourism, operational standards and certifications, managing risk, and sector challenges, opportunities and initiatives.

The chapters are interspersed with case studies and sector perspectives, including one on Sustainability and Adventure Travel in Cape Town from affiliate member, Cape Town Tourism and an opinion pice from Karen Kohler, Research Manager at Tourism KwaZulu-Natal.

Of particular relevance to South Africa's current visa debacle, is a section on 'UNWTO and Visa Facilitation', in which it states; "Joint research by the UNWTO and the World Travel & Tourism Council (WTTC), in May 2012 demonstrated that improving visa processes could generate an additional USD206 billion in tourism receipts and create as many as 5.1 million jobs by 2015 in the G20 economies."

UNWTO has identified five important areas of opportunity for visa facilitation:

1. Delivery of information
The availability and reliability of the information on entry formalities – especially visa requirements and procedures is among the simplest measures to address.

2. Facilitate current visas processes
A major opportunity for improvement is the way visa requests for temporary visitors are processed in general, as well as the requirements linked to this process. Whether these requirements are personal interviews, official documents or certificates, they usually produce at least temporary bottlenecks as well as uncertainty and long wait times. Among the techniques suitable for improving these processes are the better use of modern information technologies by service providers and the consideration of visas on arrival.

3. Differentiate treatment to facilitate tourist travel
The technique of facilitating the visa process for certain types of visitors is widely used among countries, especially for temporary visitors. The form this facilitation takes can range from easing restrictions depending on the means of transportation – for example, cruise passengers can be allowed to disembark from the ship without a tourist visa or to arrive by charter planes – to special treatment for specified geographical areas or ports of entry.

4. Institute eVisa programmes
Currently, a widely discussed opportunity is the use of eVisa. If an entry visa cannot be avoided, eVisa is the option preferred over the traditional, paper visa. It can be more easily obtained and requires neither the physical presence of the applicant nor the presence of the passport.

5. Establish regional agreements
There are already a number of regional agreements in place that allow travellers from a third country to move freely between member countries once admitted by one of the participating countries. The agreements made between the Members States of the South African Development Community to introduce a Univisa, and separately between Uganda, Rwanda and Kenya for a Tripartite Tourism Visa are a good example of this.

The Report can be downloaded at _www.affiliatemembers.unwto.org/publication/global-report-adventure-tourism_

Which Social Media Platform is right for your Business?

The social media bubble is expanding fast, with more interactive platforms coming online by the day. In this article, **Tyne van der Merwe** explains where to get started.

All social media works off the same premise...they are interactive platforms, which encourage members to join and interact with each other.

Facebook is very much focused on personal interaction and currently has over 1.4 billion members. The business element, Facebook Pages, is a great platform to market your tourism and hospitality business. It allows you to post very interactive content (text, images, video, links). You are also able to target very specific market segments via paid for advertising by 'Boosting' posts to these segments by using selected key words for as little as R10 per day.

Facebook also allows you to add Apps to your Page. A great App for the tourism industry is Trip Advisor Reviews, this creates a tab and keeps an up to date stream of customer reviews straight from your Trip Advisor profile. A great add-on to this App is the ability to create a 'Book Now' tab, directed to the booking page on your website.

Twitter on the other hand is a more real-time platform and lets you engage with your audience by sending out 'Tweets' of 140 characters in length. This is a great platform for a customer facing and servicing business.

Instagram is the new generation and is currently the fastest growing social media. This platform is based solely on images. You can attract new followers and likes by using selected hashtags such as #rhinos #southafrica #kruger which come up in their 'Explore' tab.

The key to success in social media is having a clear strategy upfront, which deals with key marketing principles and a great understanding of your product or service, the segments it needs to reach and whether it is best expressed with words or images.

For assistance with your social media, Tyne can be reached at Sprout Consulting via email at *tyne@sproutconsulting.co.za* it

if this is your idea of facebook...

...we need to talk!

Sprout Consulting will help to conceptualise and implement a sound strategic campaign for your company's social media presence.

We provide guidance and expertise on the following social media platforms:

- Facebook
- Instagram
- Twitter
- LinkedIn
- Pinterest
- Google +
- Blogs

HR | MARKETING | ACCOUNTING | IT

sprout CONSULTING
your outsourced head office

info@sproutconsulting.co.za | *www.sproutconsulting.co.za*

Avitourism: Birding in South Africa

In this article **Leon Marais** of **Lawson's Birding, Wildlife & Custom Safaris Tours** offers tips for Tour Operators and accommodation establishments who may want to attract the growing avitourism market to South Africa.

While South Africa is firmly on the map as a safari destination, many people in the travel industry are unaware that the country also attracts a fair number of international birders. These are people who spend a significant amount of time and resources on travelling the globe to see birds and other wildlife (an interest in birds usually extends to natural history in general, but not always). They visit South Africa because the destination has a rich avi-fauna component, which is well endowed with endemic and near-endemic species (these are species that are limited in distribution to a particular country and can't be found anywhere else). So, while our total bird list of around 800 species is overshadowed by a number of other countries (Kenya has around 1 100 recorded species), in terms of special birds, the birding / wildlife combination, and ease of travel, South Africa shines fairly brightly on the international stage.

Tips for Tour Operators

The desire to add a birding element onto an established tour operating business is understandable. After all, your guide knows his Kiewiet from his Lourie, so why not expand into the birding market? Well, let's first have a look at the birders themselves, to get a better idea of their wants and needs.

Know your *Intermedius* from your *Extremis*

In terms of the international birder, there are two sub-species, namely *intermedius* and *extremis*. *Intermedius* basically uses birding as a

reason to get out into some beautiful parts of the world where he or she can enjoy birds and all other forms of wildlife. The endemics and specials, and the number of birds seen are important to a greater or lesser degree, but these are never more important than the overall goal of having a good time and seeing a lot of wildlife. *Intermedius* may opt for a break during the heat of the day, and will probably enjoy a good meal and a beverage in the evenings, when he or she will discuss a wide range of subjects with his or her guide. *Intermedius* is generally pleasant to spend time with.

Extremis on the other hand, is focused on the endemics, specials and number of birds seen. Everything else is superfluous. *Extremis* likes to wake up at the crack of dawn, and bird all the way through to dinner time (where discussion revolves around birds and not much else), and then perhaps to even go out after dinner again in search of nocturnal species. *Extremis* is a 'world lister', and in the extreme form wants to visit a country such as South Africa once to see all the endemics, and then move on to the next country. Thus *extremis* doesn't lend himself to repeat business – if it's a successful tour, then he won't return, so unless you can offer him a new country to visit, that's the last you'll hear from him.

Note that *intermedius* and *extremis* hybridise readily, so you may occasionally find an extremely serious birder who still likes to have a good time while travelling in search of the next bird on his list.

▼ *Speckled mousebird*   ▼ *Common waxbill*   ▼ *Malachite Sunbird*   ▼ *Tawny-flanked Prinia*

Bird images © Bev Langkilde

So knowing your Kiewiet from your Lourie, your Mossie from your Muisvoel, is not enough to give the international birder the experience that will deliver positive Trip Advisor reviews. You need to remember that they have birded in countries around the globe with other guides and outfits, and are expecting your company to offer them a comparative experience. Your guides need to know their birds backwards, your company needs to have the knowledge to be able to set up a suitable itinerary and provide the necessary logistics. And even before you land a birder in your bus, you need to have the web presence and reputation in the first place – serious birders look for serious birding companies. That doesn't mean that it's not a good idea to train 'general' guides to be better on the birding side, but just that it requires some specialised knowledge to pull off the birding tour properly.

Tips for Accommodation Establishments

It's perhaps easier for accommodation establishments to expand into the birding market. The main thing to do is to have an accurate bird list drawn up, in English and preferably according to the latest names and classifications (these change every now and then). Stick this up on your website (you can also put printed lists in the rooms, etc), and there you go – your clients can go birding on your property. If you have enough space you can put up a few bird baths and perhaps a feeding station, put in a few walking trails, and your visiting businessman can then go birding in the afternoon after his conference. Most places have birds knocking about (the number of species will probably be surprising), so why not use them in your marketing? You may not be poised to attract the keen birders themselves, but some of your clients may be interested, and thus pleased that you can offer them some good information and a way to relax while staying with you.

Market Statistics

A 2010 study by the Department of Trade and Industry put the size of the international birding market visiting South Africa at 8 000 to 16 000 individual travellers annually, while the domestic birding market was estimated at between 21 000 and 40 000 annually. Together they were estimated to spend between R789million and R1.5billion annually on birding trips, support services and equipment. So, while it's only a small part of the general tourism industry, it's not insignificant, and, while it's harder to cater for the serious international birder (outsourcing to established birding companies is an option), many a guest house or lodge owner can benefit from putting some effort into developing the birding potential of their property, especially if they are located close to popular birding destinations.

The Department of Trade and Industry Avitourism study has information relevant to those who would like to investigate the potential of avitourism.

Download it at www.tourismtattler.co.za/downloads/dti-avitourism.pdf

▼ *White-breasted Cormorant*   ▼ *Greater Flamingo*

About the author: Leon Marais *was born and raised in South Africa and is a THETA/FGASA (Level 3) and SKS Birding Specialist Guide. He studied for a Postgraduate B Soc Sc Degree at the University of Natal and then began his guiding career in the safari industry, spending around 6 years guiding at various game reserves in South Africa, where he developed a special fondness for African mammals and predators in particular. He was introduced to the pleasures of bird-watching by his grandfather and has been looking at birds through binoculars since he was but knee-high to a Marabou Stork.*

After leaving the safari industry he joined Lawson's Birding, Wildlife and Custom Safaris as a freelance guide in September 2005 and then joined up full-time as a partner in the business in March 2007. Find out more at www.lawsons-africa.co.za / www.leonmarais.com.

Risk in Adventure Tourism

The business of providing adventure activities to tourists is a contentious issue when it comes to securing risk transfer via short term insurance. The reasons are as complex as this niche tourism sector is diverse, writes **Des Langkilde**.

Downhill Mountain Biking - image courtesy of Downhill Adventures

What is Adventure Tourism?

The Adventure Travel Trade Association (ATTA) defines adventure tourism as a trip that includes at least two of the following three elements: physical activity, natural environment, and cultural immersion. ATTA divides adventure tourism activities into 34 types, namely: archeological expedition, attending local festivals/fairs, backpacking, birdwatching, camping, caving, climbing, cruise, cultural activities, eco-tourism, educational programs, environmentally sustainable activities, fishing/fly-fishing, cultural tourism, hiking, horseback riding, hinting, kayaking/sea/whitewater, learning new language, orienteering, rafting, research expeditions, safaris, sailing, scuba diving, snorkelling, skiing/snow/sandboarding, surfing, trekking, walking tours, visiting friends and family, visiting historical sites, and volunteer tourism.

The UNWTO defines risk broadly as a situation that exposes someone or something to danger, harm, or loss. Risk can be a physical safety matter, a risk of property loss, a financial business risk, and more. In varying degrees, risk in terms of physical safety and property security is present in most adventure tourism experiences, because adventure travelers tend to gravitate both toward activities that carry some inherent risk level and destinations that may not be as developed from an infrastructure or training perspective.

From an insurance underwriters perspective, defining adventure tourism is far more complex as the definition varies according to the specific activity provided or undertaken. It is this diversity in defining adventure tourism that makes the sector so difficult to insure under an all-encompassing insurance policy as every activity has its own particular associated risks and hence safety and risk management requirements and procedures.

Many risk management models in tourism deal exclusively with the safety and physical risks of adventure tour activities. For example, in Brazil, sector operators assess risk on a formulaic scale of probability multiplied by consequences:

Risk Analysis: (RA) = Probability x Consequences

Probability runs on a scale of 1 (rare) to 5 (certain), while consequences run on a scale of 1 (no harm) to 5 (catastrophic). The minimum Risk Analysis possible – 1 (rare) x 1 (no harm) = 1 – would

be a risk that is highly unlikely to happen, and if it did occur, would not result in harmful consequences. Therefore, this outcome is a very acceptable operational risk. The maximum Risk Analysis – 5 (certain) x 5 (catastrophic) = 25 – is a risk that is sure to happen, and if it occurred, would be catastrophically harmful.

Adventure Tourism Insurance Needs

The most important risk that operators need to transfer by means of insurance is liability, which can be defined as; *the state of being legally obliged and responsible*. In a legal sense, all operators have a *'duty of responsible care'* to their clients, which implies that they must take every possible precaution to ensure the safety and well being of those for whom they are caring.

According to Wayne Forrester of Savage Jooste & Adams Attorneys, the concept of a *legal duty* is a device that courts in South Africa use in determining whether or not it is reasonable to impose liability. A tour operator therefore has a duty to conform to reasonable standards of care. The test of ascertaining the existence of a duty of care in any particular case is the *'foresight of a reasonable person'*. This means that one owes a duty of care to persons to whom harm may be reasonably foreseeable.

In this regard the following questions must be asked:

1. Would a reasonable person in the position of the defendant have foreseen the possibility of his or her conduct injuring another? and;

2. Would a reasonable person have taken steps to minimize against this danger?

3. If so, did the defendant take the steps in question? If not, the defendant would probably be considered negligent.

In the tourism industry most claims that give rise to liability are personal injury claims. It is also possible for a liability to arise under circumstances where no first aid is available or no proper evacuation plan is in existence.

The most common insurance product used for the transfer of liability risks in tourism is General Public Liability. Most of these policies are underwritten for risks associated with accommodation, food and beverage service providers. The policy wording generally accommodates incidents where the policyholder is negligent, which may arise from *'slip and fall'* incidents, such as slippery floor tiles or

Extreme Sandboarding - image courtesy of Downhill Adventures

Bloukrans Bungee jump - image courtesy of Face Adrenelin

faulty building construction, such as loose balustrades or *'food and drink poisoning'*. The majority of these policies specifically exclude incidents resulting from fee-based excursions, such as transportation, events and 'potentially hazardous' adventure activities.

Considering the Risk

Contrary to popular belief, liability insurance underwriters are not risk averse – it's just that some insurers have more of an appetite for certain kinds of risk than others. Rates are however determined on the underwriters perception of the risk, influenced both by their own claims experience and the information supplied by the broker, who in turn is influenced by a combination of their own experience and by the insurance proposal form submitted by the client.

Bearing this in mind, it stands to reason that the more concise and in-depth the information submitted by the client, the more the broker can use this information to influence the insurers' premium rating decision. Bear in mind that most liability insurance coverage is governed by re-insurance treaties, that is to say that the treaty defines the parameters under which the insurer will accept the risk being transferred from the insured. Any liability risk that lies outside of, or goes beyond the treaty will therefore have to be assessed on an individual basis and rated accordingly. It is in this process that adventure tourism operators can influence the terms favourably.

Risk Management

Being able to present a concise risk management plan of your adventure tourism business activity, or combination of activities would be the first step.

Certainly any adventure tourism operator who is able to present risk analysis documentation when applying for liability insurance would be rated as a responsible entrepreneur and be afforded more favourable insurance premiums as a result.

Group insurance schemes

Group insurance schemes are based on the principle that all members of the group share a common risk exposure profile and subscribe to set operational standards. The insurance concept; *the premiums of many pay for the claims of the few* applies here, and results in often vastly reduced premium contributions being levied on the members of the group. In these schemes, the group is normally a registered trade association that becomes the insured under the policy, which then covers its members. To obtain optimum premium rates all members would be obliged to participate in the group insurance scheme and the association would collect the pro rata premium contributions from its members and pay the insurer in a lump sum on inception of the policy.

Providing such a scheme to an Adventure Tourism Association does become problematic however. The first consideration is the diversity of activities and experiences that fall within the adventure tourism sector. From a public liability insurance point of view, the underwriting criteria adopted in rating a risk in terms of frequency of occurrence, and severity of incidence, will vary dramatically from one activity to another. Ascertaining such risks against hugely diverse activities becomes even more difficult when faced with the lack of quantifiable accident or incident reports against which underwriters are able to assess the risk. Regulatory compliance issues also impact on the provision of insurance cover, as policy wording requires that the insured abide by the laws and regulations that govern the industry in which the insured operates.

It is quite possible that the public liability insurance policies that many adventure tourism operators currently have in place may well be totally inappropriate to their specific activities, and the policy may not respond in the event of a claim.

Conclusion

Adventure tourism businesses in South Africa should be encouraged by the efforts of the National Department of Tourism in partnership with the South African Tourism Services Association (SATSA), who have been tasked by the Minister of Tourism to create a home for self-regulation of the adventure tourism sector. Once this processes is finalised, insurers will be able to structure a group insurance scheme to underwrite the liability risks of SATSA members in this category at far more favourable premium rates than are currently available.

For more infomation or advice visit www.satib.com

it

www.ingramcontent.com/pod-product-compliance
Lightning Source LLC
Chambersburg PA
CBHW050401180526
45159CB00005B/2109